EVERYDAY HEROES OF MOTHERHOOD

LOVE LETTERS TO EXTRAORDINARY MOMS

KAREN E BEMMES

Everyday Heroes of Motherhood

Love Letters to Extraordinary Moms

Karen E Bemmes

Copyright ©2016

PKBemmes Publishing

ISBN: 978-0-692-69801-3

Printed in the United States of America

DEDICATION

This book is dedicated to those who I mother by birth, by choice and by chance, to the one who made it possible for me to mother, and to those who have mothered me through the process of bringing this book to life. You know who you are, and I hope you know how much I love and appreciate you all. With deepest thanks for being part of my journey, y'all rock!

EVERYDAY HEROES OF MOTHERHOOD

INTRODUCTION

This book is a love letter to young mothers, not-so-young mothers, and mothers of all ages who are parenting the best they can. My greatest struggle in writing this book has been learning how to speak my truth and share the things that worked for me, while still being respectful to other moms out there. You see, I grew up in an era and a neighborhood where almost all of the mothers stayed at home to take care of their children. Of the twenty or so houses on our street, I only remember two who worked outside of the home. One had grown children and worked part-time. No one really judged her because her children were adults, her house was immaculate, and she was not yet a grandma. The other was a single mom, a nurse, who had lived through a horrible tragedy before I met her, whose house was anything but immaculate, and whose daughter was my friend. The judgment of this woman knew no bounds among the women in our neighborhood. When she wasn't working, she kept to herself. She read books, lots of them. I remember stacks of them sitting around the house. What I don't remember is seeing her sit outside with neighbors, joining in neighborhood conversations, or even once stepping into our home. As a child, I didn't think much about it. As an adult, I wonder what we might've done to help her, or if she even wanted our help in the first place. Was she an introvert who preferred to keep to herself, or was she sad or lonely? I hope she was an introvert who preferred her own company; if not, I hope she found what she needed after we moved away.

When I became a mom, I chose to stay home with my children in an era when it was becoming much more popular to have a career and a family. It was not an easy decision. I'm college educated. My husband is not. Ironically, he still made more money than I did at the time, and we both felt that having a parent at home with our children was supremely important. In all ways, except financially, it was the second best decision I've ever made. The best decision was marrying my husband, but we'll get to that later. Yet, I was amazed at how difficult it was to make the transition to being a stay-at-home mom. For the first time in my life, there wasn't a concrete reward for anything I did. In school, my efforts were rewarded with grades, which in turn garnered praise from my parents. Those good grades, over time, helped me get into college, graduate, and get a job. In high school, I worked and was paid. In college, I worked and was paid. After college, my efforts in every job resulted in a paycheck. It was simple. I put out effort and was rewarded with cash.

When I became a stay-at-home mom, all of that changed. I no longer work 40 hours. I was on call 24 hours a day, 7 days a week. I no longer had days off, a lunch hour, or even a commute that gave me a little time to myself. I worked harder and longer than I ever had in my life, and there was no cash reward. My only saving grace was that my husband told and showed how much he loved me and how much he appreciated what I was doing for our family. Without that, I probably would have gone stark raving mad. To complicate matters even more, none of my friends had made the decision to stay home with their children. All of my friends with only one child were still working. I felt lost and alone for a very long time and even wondered on occasion if I made the wrong decision, but when my son was about six weeks old, I was changing his diaper and dropped something on the floor. I bent over to pick the item up, and when I stood, my son recognized me and smiled. It was as if he said with his eyes, "Oh! There you are mommy!" It was one of the greatest moments in my life and the moment when I was sure I had made the right decision for me.

The key is that I made the right decision for me. I understand in the depths of my soul that my decision is not the right decision for everyone. My best friend, who I've known since we were 12 years old, could not do what I do. For her, staying at home would have been a prison sentence, and she would have been terrible at it.

In her case, working made her a better parent. She needed to have a career to be a good mom. I know at times she felt guilty about leaving her babies to travel for work, but it was the right decision for her. I also know a young woman who works part time. She wanted to stay home and tried it, but being home all of the time was overwhelming and depressing, which made it impossible for her to be a good mom. She found that getting out of the house, even for a little while, helped her be a better mom. I also know several moms who would like to stay home with their children but cannot find a way to financially make that happen. Truthfully, we made many sacrifices for me to stay home. We made them willingly, but we made mistakes, and with one income, those mistakes can become big quickly. We have dug ourselves out of deep credit card debt three times—each time the balance was larger. We had to become educated about money and have now been credit-card-debt free for over five years, while putting one and now two children through college without incurring debt for ourselves or our children.

It's important for me to clarify that nothing in this book is an indictment of any mom who chooses or needs to work. Every woman who has a child has a different view of what a good mother is, because, just in case you didn't know, there's no such thing as a perfect mother—and that's not a bad thing. All of us make mistakes, and when we are willing to admit our mistakes, especially to our children, and ask for forgiveness, we enable our children to do the same. So, to all the mamas out there, whether you stay at home, work part or full time outside the home, I salute you. Being a mom is a tough job. The job requirements change quickly, sometimes daily, sometimes hourly, and you have to keep up. There is no single right way to do it, and judgment lurks around every corner; but for those of us who've done it for a long time and done it well, there is so much satisfaction in seeing your baby become the incredible adult you always dreamed they could be. That is what this book is about—to show you that while the faces of motherhood, as well as the struggle and triumphs, may be different, every mother loves her child or children. It doesn't matter if your child is a Rhoades Scholar or mentally challenged, an Olympic athlete or cannot walk, a musical prodigy or cannot carry a tune in a bucket, the love is the same. The letters and stories in this book are illustrations that great mothering comes in many different forms. The letters are words from my heart, shared with the intent to lift the spirit and inspire all mothers to do their best, regardless of their circumstances, to raise a generation of children who make a positive difference in the world, because we've made a positive difference in their lives. It is my joy and privilege to share these letters and stories with you, and I hope these women inspire you as much as they have inspired me.

Why letters, you might ask. Why not just tell the stories of the women I admire? I chose letters because I enjoy writing them and I love reading them. I've always been a letter writer, though I never thought much about it until several years ago. I had written a letter to a junior high soccer coach at the end of the season to thank him for his extraordinary effort and for being such a great role model to my oldest son and the other players. I had written similar letters in the past, but I rarely had contact with those past coaches. However, I had the privilege of spending more time with this coach when my middle son also tried out for and made the junior high team. Just before the season started, we were the last to leave the practice field, and the coach called me over to his car. He said he had something to show me and opened up his planner. In the back was a crumpled up envelope with my handwriting on the outside. The coach said he had kept my letter and looked at it whenever he needed a lift or a reminder of why he coached. It was a huge moment for me because I had made it a practice to write several letters over the course of my children's lives. Every year around their birthdays, if someone had been particularly influential in their lives in the past year, I sent them a letter. I also write a letter to my children every year around their birthdays to talk about the year that has passed and the one coming up. I even wrote a letter to my youngest before he was born while I was in the hospital due to a high-risk pregnancy, and I wrote him another letter after he was diagnosed with a rare medical condition requiring life-saving medication for the rest of his life that also prevented him from being able to take medication for his later ADHD diagnosis. When my boys graduated high school, I gave them the letters to let them see how they grew up through my eyes. I include the struggles and the triumphs, and they get a snapshot of their history from the one who knew them best. It has also been a gift for me because, like most moms, I've found that it's easy to forget many details of their childhood. Moms get caught up in living and raising children and forget the incredible moments they've rejoiced and the hurdles they and their children have overcome. When I read what I had written to my children over their first 18 years, it showed me how much we had both grown and how much we both had to celebrate.

My history of writing letters to those who have touched my life inspired me to write this book. These letters to the people who have profoundly affected my motherhood journey are my tribute not just to the individuals they're addressed to, but also to every mother they represent. Some are filled with joy and were easy to write. Some were more difficult because I wanted to be respectful of people's privacy and pain. Some people I've known a very long time, and some I've never met in person, but all have helped me in my journey as a mom in some way. They all include an explanation that either details why I included the letter or what the person in the letter represents. Most are to one person, but a few are compilations of people I know who are very private and prefer the details of their lives to remain so, as well. I hope they all feel I have done justice to their stories. Letters are one of the ways I say, "I love you," and these letters are a way for me to say that I see the great job so many moms do, and I think it's high time someone told them. Happy reading and happy mothering!

UNLIKELY PARENTING
INSPIRATION

Dear Columbine Students, Parents, and Teachers,

Even though this is a book about motherhood and parenting, this letter would be incomplete if I didn't include the parents, students, and teachers of Columbine High School. The events of April 20, 1999, changed my life as a parent forever, even though I had been a parent for just over five years at the time. I never could have imagined the blessings in my life that resulted from the tragedy in yours. I do not make light of your pain and your sacrifice, but I hope it will bring you peace to know the good that came to my life because of what I learned that April morning and beyond. Everyone has events that change them forever; for me, the events at Columbine set me on a parenting course I might not have taken otherwise.

The first change might seem very superficial, but that day changed my opinion about students having cell phones in school. Before Columbine, I thought it was ridiculous to have a phone at school because I felt, at the time, that cell phones were for wealthy, spoiled students, and they disrupted learning. Hearing the stories about students who called their parents moments before they faced the gunmen roaming their school made me realize that if my children were in the same situation, I would want the last words they heard to be my voice telling them how much I loved them. I cannot imagine the anguish of that moment, but I pray that those who were able to talk with one another found some sense of peace.

The bigger and most life-changing aspect was how my parenting evolved because of what I learned about the perpetrators of that day. From what I learned that day and afterward, I decided I wanted to know my children well and spend enough time with them to instill the family values my husband and I wanted them to have. I decided that staying home with my children was a high priority and guiding them to know their own positive potential was my highest calling. I don't judge the parents of Dylan Klebold and Eric Harris, but the events of that morning inspired me to be an involved parent who helped guide my children to the best life I could and have them see how they could make a positive impact in this world. Perhaps both the Klebold and Harris families did that, but what they did as parents isn't as relevant to my story as who I became as a result of that day. Before April 20, 1999, I thought parenting was an organic process, and maybe it is for some parents. Without Columbine, my children would have probably had more freedom and a longer leash. Because of Columbine, we were more organized as a family with sports and music lessons and family fun nights. My children have told me that we spend more family time together and talk more than most of their friends' families; and while I know there are things I may never know about my children, I pray that we have led our children in a direction that will result in each of them making a positive impact on the world. I understand that this can change in an instant, as it did for the families affected by the shootings at Columbine, especially since I now have a child in high school and two living away at college—but for now, all is well. I have spent hours and days learning about the perpetrators of Columbine and the school tragedies that followed and realize there are no easy answers, but the awareness makes me a more mindful parent. I know that none of the Columbine parents had the opportunity to do that. I imagine that each parent wished they could talk to their child once more to say all of the things they wished they would have said before. I say them over and over again, sometimes to eye rolls and sighs, but because of what happened that day, I say them anyway.

In addition to the parents and students of Columbine, I am a better parent because of the teachers who kept so many students alive by helping them escape. They sacrificed their own safety to save others; Dave Sanders even gave his life to spare the lives of his students, children who were not his by birth. How could I offer my own children any less? Since that day, I make my children breakfast before school nearly every morning, or I take them out for a special breakfast now and then to the local doughnut shop. Some of my children are very uncomfortable riding the school bus, so my husband or I drive them until they're old enough to drive themselves. I realize that not everyone has the privilege or even the inclination to do that, but because I do, I feel it is a gift I give to my children and a way to show them my love; and we know it is a gift they may not understand until many years later. It may seem insignificant to some, but it is a tribute to those who sacrificed themselves that day.

I know it may seem difficult to believe that I learned all of that from the events of April 20, 1999, but I did. What I decided that day and what I still choose every day is to be a better person and a better parent. I refuse to make that day about gun control, because the lives lost were bigger than that. I refuse to make that day about tragedy, although there were plenty of them. I choose, instead, to honor all those who left this world that day. I choose to pray for them and pray that all who survived find peace and love. I choose to love my children with all my heart and to parent them as consciously as possible. I hope that doing so will honor everyone and bring something positive out of something that wasn't. It doesn't seem like much in the grand scheme of things, but it's the best I've got, and almost two decades later, it is still guiding and inspiring me to be better every day.

Love to you all,

As the mother of boys, I have a particular interest in the school violence that has happened in the US. When Columbine happened, I was preparing to enroll my oldest child in kindergarten. It was terrifying to think that school, which was supposed to be a safe haven for children, could be violated in such a way and by classmates some had known for years. While we have seen so many school shootings in the United States since then, that particular horror was nearly inconceivable before Columbine. Indeed, it was the stuff of horror movies like Carrie, not part of the lives of everyday people, as it is now. For me, the fate of the victims, although tragic, was not what caught my attention. Everyone could feel love for them and their families. The part that always stuck with me was what created the perpetrator. They were boys. They loved video games. Even at preschool ages, my boys loved video games. They wrestled and fussed and could be quite mean to one another. Before Columbine, I would have considered it typical boy behavior. After Columbine, I saw it as an opportunity to talk about kindness and the person we want to be in this world. It didn't stop the fussing or wrestling, but I hope it tempered the meanness. I used to let it pass when people said, "That's just how boys are," when they're being physically cruel or brutal. Now, I speak up and suggest that perhaps if we teach our boys about compassion, there would be less cruelty in the world. I have no idea if it makes a difference, but it's time for those of us who hold the future in our hands to decide what kind of world we want to live in and teach our children to be those people by becoming those people. If we want kindness, we become kinder. If we want peace, we become more peaceful. If we want love, we become more loving; and since the mothers of the world are still mostly considered the heart of the family, it only seems appropriate that that kindness, peacefulness, and love begins with them. It won't guarantee a better world, but it's a start.

ENDING THE MOMMY WARS

Dear Cindy,

I feel like I've known you forever and, in some ways, I have. We have a friendship that spans over four decades, and we're both aware how rare and beautiful that is, especially considering how differently our lives are. As I think about it, though, the important parts of our lives are the same, and maybe that's why we've stayed so close all these years. We understand each other's pain. We understand each other's triumph, and, for whatever reason, we've always been able to be happy for each other's successes. The gift of a lifelong friend is a rare thing in this modern, busy world. The gift of a lifelong friend whose life path seems so different is something to be treasured. You've taught me more than you know about accepting people with a lifestyle different than mine. You've taught me that we all struggle with our life decisions. You've taught me that a woman can be incredibly successful in her career and still maintain loving relationships with her family, but most of all you've taught me that the mommy wars that rage on in the world are stupid and unnecessary. I've learned that most moms are doing their best; and when they feel the support of those who have chosen differently, everyone benefits, whether they work outside the home or stay home, breastfeed or bottle feed, eat organic and workout daily, or eat on a shoestring budget and never step foot in a gym.

Like some of the other moms I am writing about, you asked me why I'm including you in a book about changing the world from a mothering point of view. You are included because you taught me very early on in our mothering journey that being a good mom has many different faces. I remember the day I brought my oldest child over to your house on a school holiday. He was just a baby, and I was a new stay-at-home mom. You were a full-time working mom who was staying home with your children on their day off from preschool. Each of your children had a friend over, and you were trying to get the kids to the table for lunch. They weren't listening, and you didn't want to yell. I offered to get the kids from the basement if you would get my little one in a high chair. You accepted, so I headed to the basement. I marched the kids up the steps, singing songs with them as we went. We washed hands, still singing, and got seated at the table. It was fun and easy for me, but you thought it was amazing. It was at that moment that I understood that being a good mom had more than one path and all paths of passionate moms are valid.

You and I have been friends since junior high, and we've run the gamut of life experiences since then. We both married our high school sweethearts, and both marriages ended after only a few years. We both chose better partners the second time and set about living the lives of our dreams. We have both achieved so many of our dreams and have faced so many challenges, as well. From the outside, most people would think your life is perfect; and I would say you've come pretty close, but I also know that your life isn't without struggle. You own two fantastic homes, beautiful cars, an incredible wardrobe, and several businesses. You can give your children almost anything, but you don't. You know the value of work because you and your husband have worked hard for what you have, and I have to tell you it made it so much easier when I made my own children get jobs as teenagers to tell them our millionaire friends made their children work, too.

You chose a different path than mine. You chose to work full time, and I never thought much about it until I had my first child. From the moment my son was born, I knew being at home with him was my greatest blessing and the life I wanted to live. You went to work every day, and I couldn't understand how you could leave your children. I couldn't imagine doing it every single day, and when I tried to do it part time later in my parenting journey, it tore me apart emotionally. On that day when I brought your children to the table, though, I understood everything. I could see how much you loved your children, but I could also see how being at home full time would destroy you as a human being. I could see that the very things that brought me joy, like singing silly songs with my children to help them with tasks, cooking with and for them, and hanging out with them all day would be the things that would deplete you. That day has stayed with me for decades and helped me look at moms who work outside the home in a very different way.

I now understand that working outside the house makes some women a better mom. Through you, I've seen a mom who loves her children and loves her work outside the home. I've seen your children grow into responsible, well-adjusted adults. I've seen you anguish over their struggles and celebrate their successes, just as I have mine. I've seen you question your choices, just as I have mine. I've seen you provide your children with opportunities I could not. I've witnessed moments in my children's lives that you've missed in your children's lives. Through our friendship, I've learned that we're both loving parents and our children are blessed to have mothers who love them as much as we do. I've also learned that we are lucky to have each other as friends because we've learned to appreciate each other's choices and see how blessed we both are.

I don't want your life, and you don't want mine. You love your life, and I love mine. Your life isn't perfect and neither is mine. We both struggle with what we might have done differently. I wonder if I should have worked and financially contributed more to my family. You wonder if you should have spent more time with yours. We both cried the day we dropped our oldest child off at college. We both wonder what our lives will be like when our children leave home and move into their first adult home. You live in a larger home than I do, but both of our homes seem so very quiet when our children are not there. We both love our husbands and look forward to spending more time with them when the children are gone. We have both chosen lives we love, and perhaps that is the greatest blessing of all for ourselves and our families.

We've all heard the expression, "When momma ain't happy, ain't nobody happy." In both of our cases, we are proud of our chosen careers. We love our families and our spouses, and although we have different paths, we are blessed that our paths crossed those many years ago and continue to stay intertwined today. You are the most giving person I have ever known. You give your attention to your work and co-workers when you are conducting business. You give your attention and support to your husband when you are with him. You give your attention and love to your children when you are with them, and you give your attention and friendship to me and the other women who are blessed to call you a friend when you are with them. You seem to have a super power to make people feel like they are the most important person in the world when you're with them. It is a gift I cherish every time I am blessed to be around you, and one I know others cherish, as well.

I know you'll be embarrassed when you read this because, like most women I know, you doubt how special you are, but you shine brightly in this world, and I am blessed to have the beam shine on me occasionally. You worry that you don't do enough to keep in touch with those you care about, but we understand and have no need to forgive because we enjoy every moment we do get to spend with you. Like all moms, you wonder what you could have done better, but when I look at your children, I know you've done incredibly well. I know it hasn't been easy, but you've lived your motherhood the best you could and your children are the proof that you've done a great job. Your children, husband, and I are all blessed to have been a part of your parenting path, and I am blessed to call you my friend.

Thank you for your friendship and perspective,

C indy is a hard worker and always has been. At the age of 14, she began her working life as a paid employee in food service as the salad bar girl at a local steakhouse. It was dirty and grueling work for a 14 year old, but she did it. At age 16, she changed jobs and worked in a local chicken restaurant through college, where she became an assistant manager, while graduating from high school with honors and then graduating from college with degrees in chemistry and biology, again with honors. She bought her own car when she was 16 and paid all of the expenses, including gas, insurance, and repairs. She lived at home while she was going to college, but she paid her own tuition. She has paid her dues and her way for most of her life.

When Cindy graduated, she began working in the pharmaceutical field and found she had a talent for regulatory work. Unfortunately for her, the field was filled with men who did not always respect women. Many were foreign born in countries where woman were not treated equally, and she struggled with those who had power over her salary and her time. After several years of traveling around the world, routinely working over 40 hours with no extra pay and not receiving the compensation she deserved, she decided to start her own company, doing the work for many companies that she had only done for one. In simple terms, Cindy's company helps pharmaceutical companies maintain compliance with the EPA and FDA. Her company specializes in helping companies that are not in compliance to amend their processes and correct their errors. Her work not only helps keep the companies in compliance, but also keeps consumers safe.

Cindy is a woman in business who has mastered the art of combining kindness with assertiveness. She is tall, thin, blonde, and physically beautiful, which can tend to result in being underestimated as a business woman. Having worked in a male-dominated field, however, she has conquered her industry by learning her trade so well that she can be assertive with the facts while delivering the information as kindly as possible. Telling a company that they have to recall an entire lot of a drug is tricky business, but Cindy does it with finesse. She parlays that talent to her parenting, as well.

Early on, Cindy found out how difficult it is for those with great wealth to raise children. That may seem unimaginable to those who struggle or fail to make ends meet, but when you can give children everything, it is difficult to make sure you do not give them too much. Over-giving leads to entitlement. Not only can children think their parents owe them everything, but they can also begin to think the world owes them. Teaching children a work ethic when there is enough money for them to play all of the time is a challenge. Living in neighborhoods where several parents do give their children everything magnifies that challenge. Cindy and her husband made their children work through high school, even though both children had school activities. Neither of their children was given a new car when they learned to drive. They learned to drive in an old truck that was given to them by their grandparents. When it came time for college, they were given a set amount of money. They were expected to contribute to their own education. Did it all work perfectly? Not always, but when it didn't, lessons were learned and everyone was wiser in the long run. It has, however, worked out well because, as of this moment, one child is applying to medical school and one has secured a first full-time post-college position, four months before graduating.

Cindy has shared how the challenges of working full time have affected her. She has anguished over having to disengage herself from a crying child who is begging her not to leave for a business trip. She has listened to the details of a big game over the phone, rather than watching it. She has missed parts of her children's lives that others cherish, but her career has also provided her children with incredible opportunities to travel and have unique experiences. Her children still love her and want to spend time with her. She and her husband talk multiple times per day, especially when they are away from one another. She works hard to keep her priorities straight, and her priorities love her for it. Her life isn't perfect, but it's pretty darned close, and that's all any of us can ask.

THE BEST UNLIKELY FRIENDSHIP

Dear Mary,

I don't know if there is a parent in the world I admire more than you. I know you've had your struggles. I know you've had your doubts, but I also know how dedicated you have been to raising a young man of quality who will make a positive difference in this world. I can only imagine how difficult it is to raise a son on your own. I can only imagine adding racial issues to the equation; but I have seen you ride this parenting wave with so much grace, and your dedication has resulted in exactly what you set out to do. You have raised a young man of great character who is contributing and will contribute to this world in a positive way.

The most poignant moment in our years of knowing each other happened at a soccer game. I had never seen you or your son express temper of any kind. I had never even seen either of you upset; but that day, at the other end of the soccer pitch, your son ran toward an opposing player in a way we all knew could end in trouble. His back was stiff, and his fists were clenched, and everyone watching and playing knew he was angry. The part I love about this story is that you were more confused about why your son would react that way than anyone. You couldn't understand what could make him so angry, and then I told you I could only think of one word that could make him that angry. You looked at me in disbelief until we heard your son shout at the other player to tell the referee what he had called your son. He never raised those clenched fists, but he never backed down. The wise referee sent both players out of the game, and I watched as you both paced the sidelines on opposite sides of the field until you calmed down enough to sit. I was and still am in awe of the incredible self-control you both showed that day. It is a moment in my life I hope to always remember and emulate.

That situation could have deteriorated so quickly into something ugly and brutal, but it didn't because of how you raised your son. There is no doubt that if your son had used his clenched fists, his teammates, none of whom shared his racial heritage, would have cleared the bench to support him. Nothing would have been learned and a bad situation would have become worse. Instead, your son was a role model of how to handle great adversity with grace. He was angry and had been taunted and nearly dared to lash out, but he chose to speak his mind without creating violence. It is a lesson that so many need to learn, and it was a privilege to witness.

That was the moment I knew your dedication to being a great parent was working. That's when your son proved he was a young man of quality who will make the world a better place. I was and still am inspired by that moment and your friendship. As with many friendships, mothers who work and chase kids don't get to spend as much time as we would like with those we care about. We also don't always tell those who have inspired us and changed our lives how much we appreciate them. This letter is an affirmation that I was watching, and I saw what you did, and I am in awe of the end product. You are truly a role model for those who single parent, especially for those in similar circumstances, and you are proof that good parenting can overcome bad circumstances. You are amazing.

In admiration and awe,

B y all logical accounts, there is no reason for me to be friends with Mary. She's black, and I'm white. She works full-time, and I am a stay-at-home mom. She's happily single, and I'm happily married. The only reason we met was because our sons played soccer together, and I now count that as one of the greatest blessings in my life. I've learned a lot from Mary, much more than I'm sure she ever realized until now. Mary and her son could have so easily become a statistic. When her son was small, Mary was a single African-American mom who lived in Chicago and received no help from her son's father. Mary chose to move away from her hometown and her family to give her son a chance at a better future, and although the hometown she left had excellent opportunities, she had worked in the school district our children attended and felt it would be a better fit for her son. It was a bold, life-changing event for both of them that included more than a few growing pains.

I met Mary shortly after her move and couldn't help but like her. She's friendly and has an infectious smile and laugh. I'm not sure exactly when we made the transition from acquaintances to friends, but I'm so very glad that we did. One of the things I admire most about Mary is that she has never once blamed her circumstances in life on anyone or anything. In a world where so many single moms blame their ex-husbands for their challenges, I've never heard Mary express that about the father of her child. She has been the sole caretaker of her son, and she has done it as well as she can, working her way up the ladder at Head Start to eventually running one of the largest Head Start centers in our area. This is another reason I admire her; she has not only dedicated her life to raising her son, but she has also dedicated her career to helping those in similar situations. Then, when I thought she couldn't be more amazing, she decided to leave her position with Head Start. She had passed the bar while her son was in high school and became a Guardian Ad Litem for at-risk children in our city.

I've had the privilege of watching Mary raise her son and helping her out when she needed it. I've also watched in awe as she faithfully showed up for nearly every soccer game and school events in which her son was involved. In the seven years that our sons played soccer together, I can only remember her missing two her son's games, one because she was out of town for work and the other because of a work meeting. I also know that she attended nearly every one of her son's wrestling matches through junior high and part of senior high. She was there as much a she could be, and she was there without complaint most of the time because she knew the importance of sports to her son's development in areas well beyond the physical. Even in the soccer game mentioned above, one of the fathers stepped up to walk her son to the car, and Mary realized the potential of the relationships her son was forming, not only with his friends, but with their families, as well.

Another thing I admire about Mary is how she was able to incorporate balance into her son's life. She took him to church and had him participate in the service. She found positive male role models for her son to emulate. She taught him to be proud of his race without becoming a stereotype and to be comfortable with friends of different races and cultures. What is the payoff of all those efforts? The payoff is having a son who graduated from high school with good grades, lots of friends, and a bright future. The payoff is a son who was accepted at a good college and received a scholarship for overcoming his early life challenges. The payoff is knowing that all of her dedication to raising a young man of quality was the best investment of her time.

Whenever I hear moms whine about how hard it is to raise children, I think of Mary. I think about her dedication to her son and her dedication to giving him the best possible start in life. In a world where so many spend so much time blaming circumstances, Mary never has, and the results speak for themselves. She and I have had conversations about children, relationships, and race. We don't agree on everything, but we have always been respectful of each other's opinions. I have a feeling that when Mary reads this she will be surprised to learn how much I was watching her and how inspired I have been by her, but now is the time to tell her and share her story with as many people as possible because everyone should know that every parenting moment counts.

NOTHING IMPEDES
A MOTHER'S LOVE

Dear Sarah,

Today, you shared how inadequate you feel as a mother in a post as part of a private group, where you knew there would be more support than judgment, but you were brave enough to post. As expected, the women in our special group rallied. They asked if you were taking care of yourself, and you weren't. They asked if you were drinking enough water, and you weren't. They asked if you were sleeping enough and creating art, since creating art always makes you feel better. You weren't, but that is such a small part of what happened. In addition to the basics, they shared their wisdom about boys who are almost three and throw fits because they have been denied chocolate for breakfast. They understood the meltdown, and many chimed in that they have witnessed exactly the same behavior and knew all too well the feelings of maternal inadequacy that follow. Every mom who responded had felt that inadequacy and still feels it on occasion, especially when her children find themselves in a situation that they, as the mama, cannot help them resolve. Everyone understood wanting to weep in a corner, as you said you wanted to do, and many of us have done that weeping; while children were napping, behind a closed bathroom door, or even while holding a child who had worn themselves out crying and fell asleep in our arms. We all know that feeling well. What we don't know is how you do it as well as you do.

We know that you suffer from an autoimmune disorder that you call ME in Britain and we call chronic fatigue in the US. We see you doing your best to give your son the most amazing start possible in life and doing such a good job at it, but like every mom, especially the new ones, wondering if it's enough. I laugh about that because it seems to be such a universal feeling. We all wonder if we do enough. We all wonder if we do it right, and it is only my opinion, but I think those who do wonder are the best moms of all because they care enough to ask the question. If they thought they were doing everything right, I would be worried.

What you sometimes forget is how far you've come. We met online when you were a campy, young, single girl who made beautiful bakery treats for a living. You joined a bunch of older women in a quest for a better way to take care of your home and made your way into a chat room with all of us. Maybe you didn't know how many of us envied the fact that you found this new way of being at such a young age. I'm sure you didn't realize how amazed we were that you were so talented and full of life and how much we enjoyed following your youthful, exuberant adventures in cakery and paint balling. We celebrated with you when the love of your life asked you to marry him and watched with joy as you rose above more than a few anxious moments to have a beautiful wedding and begin your married life. None of us were very surprised when you informed us just a few months later that you were expecting. What we didn't know was how huge that decision that was for you.

We didn't know that being pregnant would take so much out of you. Some of us had been pregnant before. We knew that pregnancy is tiring to the point of being debilitating at times. We didn't know that you were making a decision to be in a debilitated state nearly all of the time during your pregnancy. We knew that pregnancy sometimes led to brain fog, but for you that fog was present nearly every day. We know you would never think of yourself as courageous, but many of us thought you were. We marveled at what you went through just to have a child, and though some of us might make the same decision, it was inspiring to watch you go through the process that resulted in the birth of your beautiful baby boy. Many of us in the States wished we could have come over to love on you, bring you and your little one gifts and kisses, and/or make you a meal or two. We settled for some mailed gifts and lots of online well wishes to help you launch your parenting adventure. It wasn't an easy journey since your body was doing all the things a regular body did, but with additional ME symptoms joining the party. You struggled and persevered, sometimes valiantly and sometimes through tears, just as women have done for thousands of years, but you persevered nonetheless, and no one on this earth has ever loved a baby more than you loved yours.

I know you would never want me to say that you love your child any more than anyone else, and I would agree with you. But you love yours madly as so many of us do, and you often don't see what those of us who have been mothering for a long time do see. We know what constitutes a good mom. We can see when a mother is dedicated to creating a life that supports her marriage and her children. We can see and feel the love. Not one mother has ever done everything right, but many have done their absolute best and made it a priority to be the best she can be. You belong in that category. Even though my children are nearly raised, I am inspired by your gentle nature with your little man. I am thrilled to see that you still love his daddy. I am willing to overlook the fact that you mess up on occasion, because we all do, but the best part about messing up is getting up and trying again, which you do every time. Trying again is perhaps the best part of motherhood, because our children are so forgiving. They teach us about love in a way some of us have never seen. They love with every part of their being and aren't shy about showing it. They forgive us when we're not our best and love us just as much as they did before we messed up. They see the world in such a pure way that if we take the time to listen, we will also see the world very differently. You have done this, and you are different because of it. You've felt that forgiving love, even when you couldn't forgive yourself at the time.

I know you fear sending your bundle of love into the world where his innocence could be tainted. It's a fear so many other mothers share, but you can still have a child with a kind and gentle heart, even when the world isn't as kind and gentle as you would like it to be. Your son will see kindness and gentleness in his home and learn that he can choose it, even when others do not. He will learn the strength that kindness takes and the effort that goes into being gentle, especially when others are not; and he will be an amazing citizen of the world because of it. So, keep focusing on creating the kind of world inside your four walls that you would like to see outside of them, because your little man might just be the one who teaches others how to be gentle and kind. He might be the one to spread peace to all he meets. He might grow up to be a person of quality and kindness who is filled with a loving spirit. He might grow up to be the change you would like to see in the world, as Gandhi so eloquently put it. Maybe, just maybe, he will grow up to be just like his mom, and that would be the most wonderful thing of all.

Parenting is a challenge for nearly everyone. For those with a debilitating illness or condition, that challenge is multiplied hugely. It is estimated that over 1,000,000 people in the United States and over 250,000 in Great Britain have chronic fatigue/ME. As many as 23 million have autoimmune conditions that hinder their regular lives. Conservatively, if half of those people are women and only half of those are mothers, as many as 12 million women in the US and 60,000 in the UK are dealing with their own health issues while raising their children. That doesn't include women who are dealing with other health issues like cancer and cardiovascular disease, which include millions more. So many suffer in silence and do the best they can without complaining, which is what Sarah did for a long while.

Sarah is one of the kindest and most gentle people I've known. For those who believe in reincarnation, I sometimes think she is a flower child of the 60's who has come back to teach us about the kindness and gentleness of that era. She is filled with a love of life, family, and all things natural. Even on days when she feels her worst, she does everything she can to give her son the best of herself. Her best days include trips to the beach, the zoo, or the park. Her good days are about creating fun learning experiences for her little man in the kitchen, the yard, and with whatever learning aids she can print out, laminate, and share with him. Her bad days are filled with Disney movies and snuggles under the blanket forts she and her little man construct on the couch. Like so many other moms, she pushes herself when she should rest. She gives more than she thinks she has to give, and she puts the needs of her family above her own needs until her body revolts and requires a movie day.

To deal with her condition, she has changed her diet. She has lowered her carbs and eliminated several foods that used to be part of her everyday life as a baker. Her diet is dairy free, wheat free, and sugar free, which has helped her health immensely. No day is easy, but some are easier than others. She is an inspiration to so many with her sweetness and determination, and in the rare moments when she needs support, she knows where to get it. It took a while to develop the courage to ask for help, but Sarah has found that people are happy to help her and her family whenever they can. If I were closer, I would be happy to help her out and can only hope that one day I will be able to do that, even if just for a little while. It would be an honor and a privilege.

If you know someone with an autoimmune condition like chronic fatigue, MS, fibromyalgia, or any other debilitating condition, especially if they are a mother, reach out to them. Offer to have their little ones visit you on their bad days. Offer to go on outings with them on good days. Let them know that support is there when and if they need it. They may not take advantage of your offer, but it might be just the lifeline they are looking for.

To learn more about the conditions mentioned above, you can visit the following resources:

http://www.meassociation.org.uk
http://www.cdc.gov/cfs/causes/risk-groups.html

WARRIOR MOMS

Dear Marylin,

Although we've never met face to face, I feel privileged to have watched your journey as a mother from halfway across the world. As a fellow mom of boys, I understand your amusement with how your boys' minds work. As a fellow mom of a child with special needs, I understand how taxing it can be to put so much of your energy and focus into helping your child to live his best version of normal. What I don't understand, and yet admire so much, is how you do it by yourself. Not long ago, my husband was working out of town for six months, and with my son, I was holding down the fort by myself. While it took a while to get in the swing of things, we did finally create a new "normal" and did the best we could. I thought I was getting a better appreciation for single parenthood, and on some level, I think I was, but in the midst of that, you shared an article about how having to parent alone for a while couldn't compare with parenting alone for the long haul. At first, I was insulted because parenting alone is difficult, and I felt I was handling it rather well, but one statement in that article made me realize how much more difficult it is for single parents than I ever realized. The article reminded me that no matter how far away my children's father might be or how long he might be gone, he was still a part of my life and theirs on a daily basis. He was the voice at the other end of the phone that saved my sanity on many days and lifted me up with words of encouragement on others. Learning that was such a sobering fact and one that made me respect you even more.

My husband is my lifeline. I rely on him for so much support. You are raising your sons on your own, and other than a few weeks each year when they go to visit their dad, you are their sole caretaker. Taking care of typical boys would be enough of a challenge, but you are also tasked with taking care of a child with autism, who has come such a long way since we first "met" online. Your son has learned to eat foods he could not tolerate at one time. He learned to take a bath after years of hating it and throwing a fit every time you bathed him. He learned to, mostly, sleep through the night. He learned to laugh and smile, which is no small feat for many children with autism; and he learned to love in his own unique way, because you loved him the way he needed to be loved.

I've watched your patience level grow and grow. I've watched your frustration level steadily drop. I've watched your struggling son grow into a young man who not only has a mother who loves him, but also believes in him with all of her heart. Yes, he still wakes in the night and has moments when he cannot handle his strong emotions, but your ability to handle those moments has grown, even as the number of those moments have waned. It has been a privilege to watch you evolve and grow into a loving family that begins with a mother who loves her children with the fierceness that mothers of children with extraordinary needs understand. At the same time, I admire how you are able to balance giving your child with extra needs what he requires with giving of yourself to your son without those extra needs. Every parent worries about how they raise their children, but those who have a combination of children who do and do not have extra needs worry even more about how they parent each of their children. They know they have a child who requires more attention than the other(s) and wonder if they give their typical children enough attention. At times, they know they ask much more of their typical children than other families do. They ask them to be more mature, more understanding, and kinder than other children as they cope with their siblings, and those children comply more often than not. They ask their typical children to be more independent and sometimes to grow up faster than their peers, with a perspective of the world well beyond their years. They ask those children to take much less for granted than their peers and to understand the gift of being "normal" and so often, those children take their "normal" and turn it into something amazing. They become the child who can do it on their own. They become someone who can have more patience with our needier children than anyone could have expected. They become people who don't complain about the ordinary things that most children, teens, and sometimes even adults complain about, because they have seen firsthand what it is to struggle to live what we think is a normal life. They see it in the way their sibling works harder to do things that come easily to them, and they see it in the way a parent summons patience from a well neither the parent nor children knew existed. They see the parent do more than anyone thought was physically, emotionally or mentally possible and live to talk about it, usually with humor—often a sordid type of humor only another parent dealing with the same condition would understand. They see a parent function on too little sleep, too much bad-for-you food, and, in your case, with no other parent to tag team with when the going gets rough. They see a parent who must be firm when she wants to crumble and one who must be kind when she feels like screaming. Because they do, they see a strength that others don't see. They understand the human spirit better than most, and they become better human beings because of it. I know not every situation plays out that way, but it's what I'm seeing in yours most of the time, and I felt that you needed to know that I'm watching and cheering you on and admiring you from halfway around the world.

Too often, mothers with extraordinary children are unseen, or worse, ridiculed for the behavior of their children who cannot process life the same way others do. I know because before I had a child who processes life differently, I was one of those people. Before having children of my own, I had the ridiculous notion that everyone should be able to "control" their children and raise them like everyone else's. I'm older, wiser, and more experienced; and I've learned what a good mom really is. A good mom is one who dedicates herself to raising the best children she can, regardless of the circumstances. Life is never perfect, and with children who have extra needs, moments of perfection sometimes seem impossible, but they happen. Those moments look ordinary to other people. To them, it just looks like a bath, when it's really a little boy who had conquered a mountainous fear to sit in the bath water he has detested his entire life. To them, it looks like an uneventful trip to the store when it's really a triumphant moment of having been around a large group of strangers and lots of external stimuli without having a meltdown from overwhelm. To them, it looks like a typical childhood pout when a child has been told to put away their video game for the evening, when it is actually an extraordinary moment of compliance from a boy who usually has a strong physical reaction when he's asked to do something he doesn't want to do. Perfection comes in moments others see as normal or don't even see at all. It is a gift to those who work so hard to help their children get to that point. It is also a gift when those who are watching don't judge, but instead cheer you on, lift you up, and rejoice when normal comes along. Thank you for letting me be part of your journey in that way. Thank you for giving me perspective. Thank you for making the world a better place because of the type of mother you are. I've wished for a long time that people could know and understand your story. I want people to know how difficult motherhood can be for some, especially other mom are complaining about their typical children, who are amazing, if they will just see them that way. On occasion, I've wanted to scream at them and tell them that they have no idea how easy they have it, but I also know the folly of doing so. Everyone has struggles. Every mom has stress. Not every mom appreciates the small moments, but those with extraordinary children do, and moms like you make moms like me proud to be a part of this connection we call motherhood.

There are many women I admire who parent children with special needs. I have friends and family members who parent children with ADD/ADHD, Spina Bifida, Autism, congenital heart defects, speech and hearing difficulties, Down syndrome, mental health issues, or an assortment of other challenging life situations. Many have spent time in some type of hospital intensive care unit. All have spent time with specialists who monitor their children and, in essence, tell them how to parent their child. It doesn't just happen at the yearly checkup when the height and weight are measured. For many children, it is quarterly, monthly, and sometimes even weekly that they are paraded to doctor after doctor and specialist after specialist. It is exhausting, but often, when parading their child to the doctor or the hospital for what can seem like the millionth time and they are throwing themselves the biggest pity party ever, they encounter someone who makes them take a step back and count their blessings.

Although others might disagree with me, I believe that the Divine does not give us more than we can handle. As the joke goes, though, some days I wish the Divine didn't trust me so much. Someone once asked me why I thought my extra needs child was in my life, and he was surprised when I answered, "To humble me." My older two boys achieved easily—not that they were without challenges, but none of the challenges seemed too big to overcome. School came naturally. Learning was easy. Both are athletic and have great friendships. Nothing came easily for my youngest. I spent eight weeks in the hospital before he was born because my water broke thirteen weeks early. He was born by emergency C-section because, although he was head down and engaged when he was scanned the morning of his birth and the Pitocin drip was started, he somehow disengaged, wrapped himself in his umbilical cord and cut off his own oxygen supply. He spent five weeks in the neonatal ICU, and as difficult as it was to see him there, it didn't compare to the other infants who shared the room. He was the largest baby in the room at 4 pounds, 9 ounces/2.07 kg. His lungs were fully developed. We thought we were in the clear until he failed to grow and underwent many tests to confirm that he had a pituitary disorder that would require medication for the rest of his life; lifesaving medication that would preclude him later from taking any medication for ADHD, which was diagnosed at age seven.

Before my youngest was born, I was an arrogant parent. It pains me to say that, but it is true. I wondered what was wrong with people who couldn't manage their children and their issues. Until I had complicated issues of my own, I didn't understand how difficult it can be and the effort it takes to be a good parent to a child with extraordinary needs. It changes people, mostly for the better. It made me grow in ways I couldn't have grown through any other experience. It taught me to appreciate life and people in a way I may not have before and to focus on the spirit, rather than the trappings of the human body. It made me aware of how to help my child live up to his potential through encouragement, positive challenges, and love. It creates a warrior mom who will take on whatever and whoever gets in the way of her child's success, who will tell it like it is and take no prisoners if she feels her child is being discriminated against. Some do that quietly. Some do it boldly, but all who have those children remember the moment the warrior mom was born, and she will always be grateful for it.

I salute all of the warrior moms out there who deal with more than anyone will ever know—the women who cry behind closed doors over the struggle, as well as the triumphs, they think no one will understand. I especially salute those who do it without a life mate and take it all upon themselves to take excellent care of their children.

While I know that there are always helpers, I also know you are stronger than you think, wiser than you know, and admired by more than you can imagine. Keep up the great work.

BECOMING A SCHOOL MOM

Dear Susan,

In this book, I've included so many moms who have lived through extraordinary circumstances, but I've included you because of your extraordinary choices. Few people leave a high-paying job when they are the person providing insurance for a family with six children. Fewer still, when they return to work, take a job that pays less much less than they could have made in the corporate world and yet requires so much of them emotionally and physically. You may not see it that way, but I'm sure many others do. I'm sure they sit back in wonder as you work in what most would call a difficult situation, not because you have to, but because you choose to. That is why I chose to write about you in this book, so people could understand the choices behind your "why" and the blessings that have come from following your heart and sticking to your values.

I know you were raised in a very religious Baptist home and your dad was the choir director at your church. I know you were raised in small town in the Midwest. I know you are married and divorced, like I am, because when I left my first marriage, you gave me one of the greatest pieces of life advice I've ever received. You said I would know if I had made the right decision if I fell asleep easily and slept well when my head hit the pillow the first night away from my marriage. If I tossed and turned, I might want to re-think my decision. It was simple, practical, and wise advice, and I've shared it many times. It is also what I admire about you. You look at life in simple and practical terms.

You've worked both full time and part time, and you've stayed home through your journey of parenting both of your birth children and your four stepchildren. I've often wondered how you balance it all. After hearing how a religious retreat called the Walk to Emmaus changed your life and influenced your decision to stay home, I now know why you recommended it to everyone, even those of different faiths. Everyone should have such an opportunity to face their own priorities and ask themselves the more difficult questions about how they want to live. Your decision to stay home surprised me, and I was even more surprised when you went back to work after a ten-year absence. After our conversations about why you work with a child with special needs, instead of going back into the corporate world where you could make more money and have a bigger title, I am impressed all over again with your simple practicality and wisdom. When it all seems so complicated, everyone should have a friend who helps them boil the issues of life down to simple and practical wisdom. I am grateful that you are that friend for me.

With great affection and respect,

S usan is one of those friends who comes and goes in my life. She always seems to be there when the going has gotten tough, and I'll forever be thankful for that. Her advice when I left my first marriage was so empowering, especially since she gave it to me just a day or two before I left. We were both lucky enough to find lasting love the second time we married and have both been married to those men for over two decades.

Her approach to staying home with her second child was just as practical as her advice about leaving my first marriage. When she found out she was pregnant with her second birth child and had just been through a religious retreat requiring her to look at her priorities, she realized she was being given an opportunity to put those priorities in action. She knew how expensive daycare would be for two children, but more important, she knew if she wanted to raise her children with her values, she needed to be with them more. Even though she had a great babysitter, she wanted the greatest influence on her children to come from her, so she decided to stay home.

When, her youngest was in fifth grade, Susan went back to work to help with insurance issues since her husband is self-employed. The job that presented itself, working with a child with extraordinary needs, sounded like the best possible scenario. It fit with her children's school schedule because it was in their school system. It was considered full time and came with health benefits. The job only required Susan to be at school when the students were there, so if the district had a snow day, she did, too. When the students were not at school, neither was Susan. The job allowed Susan to be present when her children needed her to be, and it was a job with meaning—taking care of someone who needed assistance and allowing her to make a positive impact in her corner of the world.

Susan is a one-on-one aide and works with the same student as they travel through high school. Her first student attended for six years because as a special needs student, she can stay in high school beyond her fourth year. By being with her student all the time, Susan has learned her student's needs and learning style and understands the student's capabilities. She modifies assignments that are beyond her student's abilities when her student is in an integrated classroom with typical students and encourages her to push just a bit more when she's working in a more specifically targeted classroom. In Susan's words, "What's not to love about this job?"

When Susan interviewed for the job, she knew to keep religion out of the public school arena, but as a Christian, she believes all humans created by God are worthy of dignity and respect and should be treated that way. Her student is confined to a wheelchair, needs help with basic tasks like eating, and also needs assistance with personal hygiene. Susan helps with some of those duties and lets others who are more qualified handle some of the other issues. Susan helps as much as she can with all aspects of her student's care. The student is now grown to the point that Susan requires assistance with helping her out of her wheelchair. Because her student has braces on her teeth, Susan brushes her teeth for her when she's finished eating. She acknowledges that not everyone can do what she does, but she also believes her student deserves just as much respect as anyone else. Susan hopes that her attitude helped her secure the position because she is called upon to do so much for her charge, and she also hopes that other students have the benefit of having aides who are willingly and humbly called to help others.

Another big aspect of Susan's job is that she learns from her student. Although that might seem unlikely since her student has had Cerebral Palsy since birth and is delayed cognitively, the student is relatively high functioning and can communicate verbally. This has relieved Susan from the necessity of having to learn a series of nods, sounds, and movements to communicate with her student. As Susan said, because of what we view as her limitations, we understand how she could be filled with self-pity, anger, and frustration. Instead, she loves to laugh. She loves to have fun. She's game to try anything. It has been a lesson to Susan that can be applied in her own life, especially in her more difficult moments. It gives her the perspective to look at her own problems and assess them differently. It has helped her to keep her complaining in check and count blessings others may take for granted, like the simple act of being able to feed yourself any food you choose. Happy gets easier when you work with someone the world might think deserves to be unhappy, and yet they aren't.

Susan has also learned to look for possibilities where others might not see them. Susan's student will never live independently. She can be left alone to watch a movie, but she can't take care of some of her basic needs, such as preparing a meal, but there are amazing things going on with people with special needs. Her student has some computer skills. She uses a computer for her homework, and she can surf the web. She uses one finger, but Susan thinks she could potentially hold a job, not to support all of her needs, but to be useful and productive, even with full-time care.

Susan made excellent money in the corporate world and could have gone back to that lifestyle. Instead, she chose to have health care, be with her children when they're off school, and have the whole summer to run them to camp, a friend's house, or King's Island, or just be with them by the pool. She took the job for convenience and the benefits. After she got the job, she realized that she had answered more than a job opening. She had answered a Divine call to take care of another mother's child, a child who needed someone strong in spirit to advocate for her and be the "school mom" her child so desperately needed.

As mothers, we all hope we will raise children who will change the world in a positive way. Most of us know that in order to do that, we have to step up and change ourselves and show our children by example. Susan gave up the corporate world to raise her kids in a hands-on fashion, teaching and showing them how to live and make a positive difference in the world. As she returned to the world of paid work, Susan chose a job that aligned with the values she and her husband taught their children. She hopes that beyond the grateful notes she has received from her student's parents, who deeply appreciate her dedication to their daughter, her own children will understand the value of choosing a life of service to others. I've met those children and have known one since birth. I'm sure they're watching; and even though they may not show it, I'm sure they are taking notes of their own.

THE SPIRIT MOM

Dear Kristi,

I knew you were a kindred spirit when I saw you holding a book written by Judith Orloff. Even though I hadn't spent a lot of time with you, I could tell you were a person of deep faith, not in a rules and regulation of religion way, but in sharing the love of your perception of God. I love how you call yourself a "Metholic" because you were raised Methodist but now practice in a Catholic church, while teaching your children about your religious upbringing, as well. I also love your idea that God is always with you in your daily journey and that you find God in the questions of life. I find it interesting that instead of looking for answers, though, you spend your time and energy bringing goodness and love to life.

I know your search for a church was not easy; and when you found your church, it felt like home. I love how you heard the call to become a full Catholic member of your church, which you did, and then became a Healing Touch practitioner because of it. Talk about a clash of cultures. It's not often that a "new age" practice like Healing Touch is associated with a religious organization known to be as rigid as the Catholic Church. It was through talking about your Judith Orloff book and healing touch that we connected, and I'm so glad we did. When you talked about Healing Touch, I could see the joy in your eyes and feel the peace in your words as you spoke about a practice to help others heal. I reveled in hearing about how you learned to listen to your intuition through Healing Touch and were able to receive Divine guidance through the messages of others. It was how you figured out to have your adrenal glands checked when someone in one of your workout classes found out that hers were not okay.

I was shocked and dismayed when I learned you had to put your Healing Touch work on hold because of your own health issues, but was so pleased that you had the strength to find yourself and your balance in the silence as you distanced yourself from everyone else's needs and tended to your own. When we talked about you being a part of this book, I didn't have the words to tell you how much it meant to me to have you share your journey, because I am sure I was on the verge of my own adrenal breakdown. I was looking for confirmation that what I was about to embark on was okay, and you gave it to me. You talked about spending time in silence, talking to and listening to the Divine guidance, and how at peace you were with giving up the busyness moms can become so wrapped up in. You gave yourself permission to heal and forgo busy, and it worked. Your outlook on life and ability to find inspiration in a sunset or the sound of a bird inspires me to find the joy in the every day. Your ability to assimilate the serenity of Buddhism and the hospitality of the Jewish faith encourage me to do the same. Your ability to see the blessing in your daughter's unplanned pregnancy by seeing the strength and beauty in her inspires me to see the good in my own children.

Like so many others, you were surprised when I asked to interview you for this book, but because of your challenges and how you handled them, I felt the book would be incomplete without you. You've faced your sister's cancer with her and feel grateful for her healing. You've faced your own health challenges and used them as a way to learn about yourself and your faith and come out stronger and more loving on the other side. What better lesson can we learn as moms than to put our family's needs at the top of our list, knowing that we need to include our own needs as part of that priority? You are a wonderful example to us all that life rarely goes as planned, but regardless of the challenge, we can find beauty, grace, and blessings in all of it. Thank you for being so humble and willing to share your journey. It has blessed me more than you'll ever know.

In love and light,

K risti was born in a small Midwest town and raised in a home of deep faith. Her relationship with the Divine has always been the guiding force in her life, although like many, she stepped away from church during her college days, but she maintained her spiritual connection with the Divine throughout. Kristi's call to serve came through her choice of profession, which was to teach kindergarten. She met her future husband about a year after she graduated college, and it wasn't long before they were planning a family. Kristi's husband, Tom, had been raised Roman Catholic, and it was important to him to raise their children Catholic. Kristi, who had been raised in the Methodist faith but believes that God is bigger than any one religion, agreed, with the caveat that she would be able to share her faith journey with her children, as well. It became a family joke that Kristi is a Metholic, raised Methodist and practicing Catholicism. That decision helped Kristi learn more about what she really thought and felt about God, religion, and her own beliefs. She learned what was important to her and what wasn't. Most important, she deepened her belief that God is in the questions of life. It isn't about the answers, although they come. It's about the journey and the questions that arise through the journey that can lead one toward or away from God.

Every day, Kristi lights a candle and asks the Divine to help her to continue to see the beauty and blessings in her life and in the world. She feels called to bring goodness and light to the world, and she lives in gratitude every day. She has deepened that faith through her sister's rare abdominal cancer, which resulted in her sister adopting two wonderful children after having given birth to one child of her own. As her sister puts it, she had one child through her womb and two through her heart. It helps Kristi understand that through the challenges of life, there are blessings and gifts and people can learn more about themselves in those challenges than they could have ever learned otherwise. Although it's a natural tendency to try to protect oneself from the challenges of life, Kristi believes that facing those situations through faith is always the better choice, because she sees God as love and the challenging situations in life as an opportunity to love one another.

One of the ways Kristi chose to love others is through a practice called Healing Touch. It was through her church that Kristi learned about Healing Touch, but it was a long journey to get there. In the beginning, when Kristi and her husband began attending church together, the ritual of the Catholic Church was so foreign to Kristi. She missed the familiarity of what she knew, and the church they attended didn't feel right, so she and her husband kept looking. Eventually, they found their church home and settled into her new Divine space. She considered herself a non-Catholic member of the church until one Sunday, about four years after she began attending mass at her church, when she realized she hadn't been taking Communion because she didn't want to break any church rules. That Sunday, she felt the call to take Communion. It was as if the Divine told her that the only force keeping her in her seat was her own fear of breaking a church law, instead of living in the faith that all are called to the Communion table. Kristi asked for a sign—if she was supposed to take Communion that day, she asked God to bring her husband, who was serving as a Eucharistic minister for the church that Sunday, to her part of the church. Her husband did come to her part of the church, so she got up and took Communion in the Catholic Church for the first time.

That moment was an awakening for Kristi. It taught her to listen to her intuition and trust that she could be called directly by God to take action. It took six more years before she decided to become a full member of the church. She had been through the classes to convert but had never made the final commitment. She had worried about not believing everything. She had thought about the differences in how she was raised versus what she was learning, but after her moment of clarity and her first Communion, she felt differently. She realized that many of the people who were raised Catholic had questions about their faith and weren't sure if they agreed with everything the Church espoused. Her hesitation to become a full member of her church had nothing to do with God. When she understood that and knew she wanted a deeper relationship with God, she made the decision to become a full member of her church and took the action to do so. Rather than seeing it as a conversion, she sees that decision as an extension of her ever-developing and deepening relationship with God.

Through her Bible study classes, she met several women who were involved with something called Healing Touch. Healing Touch is based on using energy to provide comfort and relief to those who are suffering, especially when other methods have failed. It is an accredited practice that is used in hospitals and medical facilities around the world. Kristi felt called to learn more about Healing Touch and how she could help others, but it taught her to help herself. She wanted to be a healing force for others, but her intuition told her she needed to take time to heal herself first. Kristi learned to listen to her own intuition and the intuition of others. One day at a workout class, one of the women was talking about having her adrenal system checked, and Kristi felt the nudge to have her own adrenal system checked, as well. She did and found that she had Cushing's syndrome, which occurs when a body has too much cortisol. In Kristi's case, the Cushing's was due to a benign tumor on her left adrenal gland, which she had treated at Cincinnati's UC Health and the Cleveland Clinic. The treatment for her personal health issues taught Kristi to take time for herself.

Kristi is a doer. She was someone who was always on the go and helping others. Through Healing Touch and helping others, though, she realized she was neglecting and depleting herself. She began to understand that she needed to take time away from her Healing Touch practice to heal herself so she could be a better wife, mother, and whatever else she decided to be in the future. Stepping back taught her to listen to her own body and her intuition. It taught her to balance busy with solitude. It taught her to be still and much more aware of what is going on around her. Kristi is now inspired by the everyday moments in life. She is inspired by nature and the human condition. She continues to read and learn about other people and religions. She is inspired by people who overcome, including her own children, who have faced their own difficult moments. Her life isn't perfect. She isn't perfect, but she's learning to be perfectly at peace with whatever comes her way.

UNEXPECTED TURNS OF MOTHERHOOD

Dear Veronica,

You are living proof that rebels and visionaries come in all shapes and sizes and that people who disagree on even the biggest issues can be respectful in the process. I miss your lunches, which were full of diverse personalities and backgrounds, lively conversations, and lots of laughter. You are one of the reasons I love living where I do because you bring women of different cultures together so we can find out that, no matter what we believe in otherwise, we all believe in being good mothers.

One of my favorite and most informative memories of how to parent a budding adult child came from one of your lunches. We were having a great time when you announced that both of your daughters, one who would have been a sophomore at a very prestigious university and one who had been accepted to some of the finest programs in the country, would be taking a *gap year, instead of pushing through with their education. Some of us already knew, and some didn't, but you could almost feel the terror sweep the room. So many of the women in that room—okay, all of the women in that room—believed in the power of an education. The idea of any of our children not attending college was unthinkable. The reactions ranged from shock to sympathy to denial, and one reaction and your response to it is still etched in my memory. I remember one mom saying that you had to force them to go, and you tried to laugh it off, but the mom wouldn't be put off. She insisted that you needed to force them to go to college, to which you responded that they were 18 and 19 and you couldn't force them to do anything. The mom pushed further that you should do whatever was necessary to make them attend college in the fall, and I will always remember your response. You told the mom that you were not going to spend $110,000 a year so your children would be miserable. It would be a waste of their time and your money. I know that conversation was not easy for you. I know you struggled with your daughters' decisions, but I still admire your courage to share it and, more important, to support your daughters, even when you weren't sure they were making the best decision. It wasn't until much later that I learned that your daughters were more like you than I had ever imagined.*

It has been more than five years since that lunch. Much has changed since then. You've moved out of our school district, and I miss seeing you on a regular basis. We're both looking at the end of our daily mothering soon, and again you've inspired me as you return to college to get another degree and pursue a new passion, rather than fade into the background. You've helped show me that although we both started late with our children, we have much more to give, not just to our families but to our communities, the world, and to life. I know you are still re-defining yourself and deciding where to best use your talents. I'm excited to see where you are headed and what it will inspire in me and in your children. You probably had no idea I was watching and learning so much, and knowing you, the credit would be put elsewhere, but everyone needs a friend like you who challenges them to be better in every way. I thank you for being that friend.

In humble gratitude,

Sometimes the greatest gift we are given is the gift of someone who opens our eyes to a new reality. Veronica is one of those people for me. We are different in so many ways and got to know each other through school activities and while our sons were on a Lego League team together for four years. Our lives have intersected in some of the most interesting ways. Our oldest children both played tennis, although hers was a daughter and mine was a son. Some of our children are musicians, although they've never played together, except when her daughter was teaching my son how to play the oboe, a program she quit, which left an opening for an oboist that my son offered to fill. Our children who graduated in 2012 were better friends and spent more time together than either of us knew at the time. When I decided to write a book on motherhood, I knew she had to be included because she has raised extraordinarily talented and intelligent children who have made some extraordinary decisions, and I wanted to know why. Veronica is a great example of walking your own path, and after learning her story, I understand why.

Veronica is the only child of college professors. Her father's family all had PHDs and were academically driven, and all of the women in her mother's generation were career women. Staying home to raise children was not something that happened in her family. Veronica was taken care of by a housekeeper and her paternal grandmother, and it was her grandmother who greeted her when she got off the bus and provided nurturing in Veronica's youth so her mom could pursue a career. Veronica's mom earned a PhD at the age of 49 and changed careers, becoming a professor. As Veronica puts it, her mom was quite determined and admirable in her pursuit of academic and career excellence. When the time came for Veronica to go to college, the expectations were high that she would go to an Ivy League school and become a doctor or a lawyer, because that's what every good Asian child did at that time. Although she went to an Ivy League school, Veronica determined that she was not going to become a doctor or a lawyer. She didn't know what she wanted to do, and the idea of working instead of going to college was something that successful Korean Americans didn't even think about; so Veronica headed off to college and went to the University of Chicago business school to major in finance. She got her MBA at the age of 24 and was hired by a major corporation to work in their treasury department, from which the future CEOs and CFOs of the major corporation generally arose. It was a place of great arrogance and privilege with $100,000 salaries being the norm for 26 year olds in the 1980s.

Unaware of the great privilege under which she was living, Veronica continued to enjoy her work and focus on her rise to better positions and the half-million dollar salaries that were in her future. She got married and moved to Europe, where she and her husband worked hard on their careers, but as age 30 approached, Veronica figured it was time to have children. It wasn't a decision made from longing for a child because she had never really been around children before. She had little to no experience with children, but she got pregnant and delivered her first child. Having that child changed everything. Veronica was astonished that she had created a little life that was totally dependent on her. At the time she became pregnant; Veronica and her husband were living in different countries and pursuing their careers. They only saw each other on weekends, but when Veronica was seven months pregnant, she took a leave of absence, moved in with her husband, and had the baby. At the time, Veronica had no support system. She had no family and no friends to help her. The Internet didn't exist so she was isolated and alone with her new baby girl, with only a few books to guide her on her parenting journey. A year and a half later, she had another baby girl and was fascinated with the idea of creating the family she never had growing up. A couple of years later, Veronica and her family moved to London, and her husband lost his job, so Veronica re-entered the workforce with her former employer and picked up the fast track she had laid down a few years before. Her commute was an hour each way. To put in her minimum ten-hour day, she would leave at 6:00 a.m. before her children got up and return at 6:00 p.m. as they were going to bed. Saturdays were spent re-acquainting herself with her children, and Monday the process would begin again. A year and a half later, Veronica's husband got an opportunity to work in Asia. Veronica decided to stay home since it was difficult for women to work in Asia at the time, and that is when her third child was born. After three years in Asia, when the children were seven, six, and two, they decided it was time to move back to the United States so their children could get to know their grandparents.

With plans to return to New York, Veronica was looking at returning to her former employer when her husband got a great opportunity in Boston. At that point, Veronica and her husband decided she would be the primary parent, amidst great pressure to go back to work from friends and family, and her husband would take the great opportunity he was offered. Veronica figured she would get the children settled into their life in America and then find work after a year or so. In the meantime, she would get re-certified for the positions she would need to go back into the world of finance. Her former colleagues had all continued with their careers and were living the million-dollar lifestyle Veronica knew she would have been living if she had stayed in the States, and her plan was to pick up that lifestyle as soon as she could. In 2002, just eight days after picking up her daughter at a friend's house and discussing a kitchen renovation with the friend's mother, the friend's mother died suddenly at age 42, leaving behind twin eight-year-old girls. That moment changed Veronica's life. Up until that point, it seemed to Veronica that people died because they were old or sick. They knew it was coming. This woman had no idea. She had plans. Veronica had plans. What if she were to die? How would she want to spend the last 24 hours of her life? She knew at that moment that the idea of returning to her career in finance was gone. She wanted to spend as much time with her children as possible, supporting them in their individual paths and exposing them to as many opportunities as they could. She exposed them to music lessons, tennis lessons, and whatever else they were interested in. Her focus was to make a difference in her children's lives and help them start with a leg up on life, and she did.

From the time she was small, Veronica was interested in helping people. As a preschooler, she asked if she could bring homeless people to her home, but that desire to help was put out of her mind as a young person because of the pressure and drive to succeed financially. As her children grew and needed her daily input less, Veronica felt the tug to help people again. She began to volunteer. She went out of her way to be inclusive and help people whenever she could. That was how she got the idea for her lovely lunches. She realized how busy everyone was and how much they needed a break and was only too happy to provide that two-hour window where moms of all types could spend time together and just enjoy themselves. It also provided an opportunity for women of different cultures, religions, and socioeconomic backgrounds to realize that, regardless of the way each one was raising their children, there were always struggles. The background may be different, but the goal was the same: to do the best possible job in raising the children they loved so dearly. For Veronica, that meant letting her children choose their own paths and not imposing on her children her own way of doing everything. It has been stressful to do that at times, because her children have not always made the same choices she would have made or the same choices she would have chosen for them. Many of those decisions have been life altering, although none have been life threatening. The kids are fine, and so is their mother. In fact, while the children were in the process of deciding who they wanted to be, Veronica was in the process of deciding who she wanted to be when her children were gone. She decided she wouldn't be one of those women who faded quietly into the background. She decided to be a person who makes a difference. At first, she chose to move toward healthcare because she felt the need to help people when they are most vulnerable. She didn't choose healthcare administration, which could line her own pockets with more money. It wasn't about the money, and as she looks back, she realized it never was. For Veronica, it's about making a positive difference in this world, and that's why she chose to work as a liaison between those having surgery and their waiting families. She updated the family periodically, rather than having them wait until surgery was over. In addition, she worked as a liaison between patients and hospital administration, sharing compliments and issues from the patients with the hospital administration. Through that experience, she learned that people, especially when they are vulnerable, are basically all the same and they were scared, especially when they were alone.

Around the same time, Veronica became involved with two nonprofit organizations: one that helped underserved women and children and one that focused on children, especially those who were homeless. She wasn't sure of which direction to direct her talents, but a personal issue helped her define her life more clearly. Veronica's mother became ill. As an only child, Veronica took on a large part of helping her mother navigate the medical profession and in doing so, became disgusted with the medical establishment. Instead of having a medical professional who could coordinate care for her mother, the responsibility to fell to Veronica and her father. It was a difficult time, but one that taught Veronica some valuable lessons. First, she learned to stop trying to control events in her life over which she had no control and to make the best of every situation. At the time, she was helping care for an elderly, sick parent, continuing to care for her family, whose home was 900 miles from her parents' home, taking graduate classes online, and serving on the board of two nonprofit organizations. It was a stressful time, but as often happens in stressful times, Veronica sees how her difficulties have made her stronger and more capable. It has changed her life in other ways, too.

Veronica is now grateful for everything. She knows some things in her life could be better, but she understands even more deeply that nearly everything in her life could be worse, much worse. She wants more than ever to give back, especially to those who were born into less than ideal circumstances. She believes that she had the good fortune to be a winner in the lottery of birth and did nothing to deserve the good fortune she was given. Because of that, she feels called to help children who are born into challenging circumstances. By helping them overcome their unfortunate beginnings, she hopes the ripple effect will be that everyone she helps will reach adulthood with better prospects for a happy, productive life. She has even signed on to become an advocate for those who need more hands-on, one-on-one help. Veronica has learned and taught others that the journey goes on, the need for mothering is eternal, and the skills she used to raise her own children can now be used to help those whose mothers were not so lucky in the birth lottery. The luckiest children of all will be those whose lives she touches—of that, I am sure.

A MOTHER'S COURAGE

Dear Dancy,

You've been through more than most mothers in my part of the world could even imagine. I wish I knew how your life was when I first met you. I wish I could have helped you through a time so difficult that no mother should have to endure it. Slavery was abolished in this country on December 6, 1865. Everyone knows that slavery is illegal. What we don't know is that it still goes on, not just in our world, but in our country and sometimes even in our neighborhoods—our suburban, Midwest neighborhoods. I'm not talking about the sordid kinds of sex slavery that the news reports. I'm talking about using the labor of honest decent people to make fortunes without ever paying those people for their efforts. I don't know why we don't hear more about this type of human trafficking, but I will be telling people about this as long as I think it might exist.

I remember when I met you and thought you were different

from the other moms I knew from India. I remember how you would sign up to volunteer and sometimes not show. I remember how frustrated people would get when that happened. I remember actually saying to one of them that we didn't know what was going on in your life, and since you didn't have a phone, what was going on might not be so great. Not great is an understatement, and I am amazed that you were able to volunteer at all, especially when you had to listen at times to the whining of those who had everything you wanted and more.

I cannot imagine the courage it took to leave everything you knew and bring your family to the US, even with the opportunity you were offered by people you thought were friends. I can imagine how easy it was to be convinced by the man you called Mr. Nice when he said he would sponsor you and train your husband to manage a business for him because friends were like family in India. In order to give your children opportunities they could not have in India, it's easy to imagine that you agreed to come here, despite your hesitation to leave your homeland, for the opportunities, education, and a life bigger than the one they could have in India.

I learned from you how people are brought into this country legally, with money they have raised to pay traffickers to "sponsor" their immigration to the United States, which was backed with promises of lucrative employment. Because of the gratitude the immigrant feels, they do not question what is happening, at least for a while. Even when they do, the traffickers lie about visas, immigration rights, and the police and tell the immigrants that if they go to the police, they will be jailed or deported and sent home penniless and in shame. I learned how traffickers work together, owning restaurants and shuttling people between them so no one will question them. I learned how people are hidden away from society and made to live in awful living conditions through an elaborate system of owning legitimate businesses that the traffickers buy and sell among themselves to avoid suspicion and prosecution. It allows the traffickers to get very rich, very quickly because they have no labor costs, Social Security, unemployment, or insurance to pay. They are even smart enough to buy at least one storefront with an apartment or two attached, so they can house the workers cheaply and always keep an eye on them while they barely feed and clothe them. The traffickers heap guilt upon the immigrants for the food and shelter and tell them they should be grateful for what the sponsor is doing for them. The traffickers create an atmosphere of fear by telling the immigrants that if they talk to anyone, they will be arrested, handcuffed, and sent to jail. It is a humiliation the immigrants avoid at all costs, and it keeps them from seeking help from the very authorities designed to protect them. In addition, most of the immigrants save as much money as they can to pay for items they will need when they come here. I also learned that traffickers know how to manipulate the people who trusted them by taking their money to save them from being robbed. Little do they know that by handing over their life savings, they have just given themselves over to modern-day slavery. In addition, I learned that the traffickers charge the workers for living expenses, which cost more than the immigrant makes; thus, they are forever indebted to the trafficker/sponsor. It is truly the American dream turned nightmare.

I learned from you that most of the immigrants that end up in this situation have come here alone. They have no one to lean on and no one to confide in. Without support, they exist in this horrendous system for years and possibly their entire lives. The stress is unbelievable, and the threat of violence is constant. It is dangerous business to try to leave this life. It takes a huge support system to help people get out of this system, and asking for help is something that the immigrants are taught is more dangerous that the life they are living. Many lose hope. Even if they try to leave, they are threatened at gunpoint, like your husband, Harold was. Immigrants are led to believe that they would be treated like criminals and are always terrified.

You explained that the tipping point for you came when someone called Family Services, telling them that you and Harold were not taking care of your children. That was when you finally said enough was enough and asked for help. As you told me, Dancy, the traffickers had promised you the moon but had given you dirt. Even when you asked for the money you had given them, they denied you had given them anything. Fortunately for you, one of the paid chefs in the restaurant where you were working, who had come to the

*United States as an illegal, helped you. He took advantage of
an amnesty program and applied for and got his green card.
He told you to get out and leave. Although Mr. Nice had his
lawyer threaten you with being arrested and deported and
despite being terrified for your lives and your children's lives,
you finally decided to go to their local police and tell them
about your situation. The police assured you that unless you
committed a crime, you would not be arrested. They gave you
information to contact the Department of Labor and even
contacted the investigator who asked you to come to his office
immediately. The investigator was leaving town for a month at
the end of the work day, so if you wanted to give your
statements, it would have to happen that day. The chef who
encouraged you to talk to the police took you to the
Department of Labor, which launched an investigation that
confirmed everything you told them; and when the owner was
informed that he was under investigation, he sold the
restaurant where you were working.*

*As good as it felt to be vindicated at that point, you lost
everything; your livelihood and home, as pitiful as they were,
no longer existed. Instead, you found out that Mr. Nice had
taken a loan out for $10,000 in Harold's name and because
he had signed for the check, he was legally responsible. With
no full-time employment and only odd jobs to support the
family, it was difficult to provide for your family, but through
your church, you found a local program that helped families in
need. That is where you met your immigration angel, Jodi. She*

walked you through the process of leaving slavery and finding freedom. You were in the country legally but someone else had all of your documentation. Because of your status, you were not eligible for welfare or any of the other services afforded to American families. In addition, the traffickers cancelled Harold's visa, so he could not legally hold a job. They even went so far as to drain the money from your bank account because the traffickers still had access to it. Soon after, you finally contacted End Slavery. Jessica at End Slavery knew exactly who to contact about human trafficking to help you get out of your situation.

Even before talking with the authorities, one of the first people you and Harold told about your situation was the principal of your sons' elementary school. It was winter, and after receiving a note suggesting that your children needed winter coats, you decided to risk going to jail, being deported, and returning to India in shame to tell the principal that you had no money to provide for your children, although you were terrified of what the principal might do, fearing that she would expel your boys. Instead, she immediately put the children into the free lunch program, which meant the children would be fed lunch and breakfast at school. Dancy, I know that knowing your children would be fed was a huge blessing for you as were the winter coats the principal gave you for the boys. Most important, she helped you contact local programs that could help with food and rent, as well as other people who assured you that you were in the country legally and would not be deported. You were still scared, but you talked to people who could help you and finally began getting the help you so desperately needed.

One of my favorite parts of your story is what happened when the word began to get out about what you had been through. Friends and neighbors began to reach out to in poignant and emotional ways. Gift cards would show up in the mail in envelopes without return addresses. A Jewish neighbor bought you a Christmas tree, made sure the children had gifts, and gave you sweaters to keep you warm in the winter. Through a local course, you were able to save money and with a matching program, you purchased your first home, closing on the home on your birthday. When you finally bought your home and hosted a party for all of the people who had helped you, you proudly gave everyone a tour, including the still empty bedrooms that provided a safe, if not extremely comfortable, place to sleep. The next day, you found out the sheriff's wife had called everyone at the party to chip in and the group had purchased beds for all of you and not only delivered the beds, but put them together for you, as well. As Christians, you asked your priest to bless your home; and after he did, he asked why there was no table for dining. Harold explained that you were saving up for furniture and that having your own home was enough. The next day, a truck came with a dining table and four chairs that to this day, you highly value as a gift from the church and from God.

You are finally in a place where you feel like the American dream is possible for you. Your children are taking advantage of their educational opportunities. Your family gives back by volunteering at a soup kitchen and through your church. You are such grateful and humble people and are sharing your story to give other families hope and create awareness that human trafficking happens, even in the best neighborhoods. You are dispelling the notion that all immigrants live frugally here and send their money home so that they can retire wealthy off of the American system. In many cases, you know those immigrants are living in poverty and fear and need help. I am honored to help spread the awareness.

When I heard your story, I was angry; and as a writer, I wanted everyone to be more aware of what's going on. I don't know if sharing your story will help anyone get away from a bad situation, but we can try. I cannot tell you how much I admire your courage to take the first step and trust someone to help you. I can hardly express how happy I am that you found the right people to help you escape an incredibly difficult and even dangerous situation. I can tell you that I admire you and your family so much for how you have lived since you were given a true opportunity to live the American dream, and I only hope your story will continue to inspire others to be more aware and take action to help others who might be in a situation like yours. Not all true American heroes were born here. I know two who were born in India, and I am humbled by their courage and strength and by how they give back in gratitude for their blessings. I am blessed to know you, to know your story, and to share it with the world. May your life from here on be filled with joy and success for you and your incredible family.

Slavery used to be a lawful institution. In the United States, slavery was officially abolished on January 31, 1865 by the 13th Amendment to the Constitution. It states: Neither slavery nor involuntary servitude, except as a punishment for crime whereof the party shall have been duly convicted, shall exist within the United States, or any place subject to their jurisdiction. If you know anything about American history, you know that is not the end of the story, but that discussion is for another day. Suffice it to say that forcing others to work without pay is illegal in the United States, but it still happens to adults, children, and families. Everyone needs to be aware.

So often in news reports on human trafficking, the story focuses on young girls and boys who are sold into sexual slavery. It is a horrible crime on so many levels, but slavery doesn't end there. It is estimated that there are 35.8 million slaves worldwide and 60,000 in the United States. While some are controlled by pimps, many are working in mines, factories, hotels, and restaurants according to the Walk Free Foundation, www.walkfreefoundation.org, founded by Australian billionaires Andrew and Nicola Forrest.

There are signs to look for. If people are being moved from a restaurant to a home or apartment in a group, there is cause for concern. If a group of men, especially young men, are working for one man who speaks English and makes all of the decisions for the group, it is cause for concern. If you try to speak to someone, and someone else intervenes and refuses to let you talk with the immigrant, contact someone immediately if possible. In addition to calling local law enforcement, in the United States, you can call the National Human Trafficking Resource Center at 1-888-373-7888, or contact End Slavery Now at www.endslaverynow.org, or call the US National Tip hotline at 1-888-373-7888. End Slavery Now is partnered with the National Underground Railroad Freedom Center. They also have a hotline database for other countries that you can access at www.state.gov/j/tip/rls/other/2011/168859.htm.

MAMA, GABBY, AND
HER GUARDIAN ANGEL

Dear Maria,

When writing a book on everyday heroes of motherhood, I knew I would have to include the story of your family because nothing is more heroic than creating a life of joy when you have suffered the loss of a child. There are more people than I care to count who are determined to never get over the loss of a loved one, no matter what the circumstances, which makes your story all the more uplifting and inspiring.

One of the blessings of having children is watching them form friendships for the first time, as we did with ours. To think that our children have been friends since kindergarten and will finish their high school careers still friends is amazing and rare. Perhaps it's luck. Perhaps it's good parenting, but whatever it is, I am grateful that Alex has been part of Andrew's journey and Andrew has been part of Alex's. I am even more grateful that I've gotten to know you and your story, because it gave me a new perspective on a subject I hope I never experience.

To some people, I know that last statement might sound cold and unfeeling, but I know you would never want anyone to suffer the loss of a child like you did. What you would want them to know is how you healed and made the world a better place in the process. You confirmed that people can heal from the most tragic of circumstances by taking positive action and living in faith. It is a lesson I'll always carry with me, and one I've shared often.

I don't remember the first time I heard your story, but I know it changed me and how I look at suffering and tragedy. I've always been a person who believed that good can come from any situation, no matter how tragic, and your family is proof of that. I've heard stories of other parents who have lost a child or multiple children who have found a way to peace, but it means so much more when you see it in person, and it's more inspiring than you know.

Because of you, I whine less and parent better, and although I don't know how much we'll see each other when our children graduate and move on with their adult lives, I know that my life is enriched and my outlook on life is improved from knowing you. I know that healing is possible. I know that good can come from bad, and now you know that your journey has been a blessing to me. Thank you for that and for so much more.

W hen you are a mom, you make some friends on your own and some friends because of your children. My friend, Maria, is one of the friends I've made because of one of my children. I met Maria when our sons were in kindergarten. Our sons are now in college and are still friends. Fortunately, I also became friends with Alex's mom, Maria.

For some women, the decision to stay home with their children is an easy one. For women like Maria, who spent years of her life studying to be a doctor, that decision isn't as easy at all. There is enormous pressure from the medical community to be fully immersed in your career. Many two-physician families have nannies, housekeepers, and various other people to keep their lives running efficiently. Maria chose a different path. Maybe it was her small-town upbringing that led her to make the decision. Maybe it was her Christian values. More than likely, though, I think it was a combination of those two things, plus the fact that Maria is one of those moms none of us wants to be. She is a mom who lost a child—a baby born too sick to live. Baby Holly was born in December. She was the third child for Maria and her husband, Stewart. Holly was born with a rare genetic condition and only lived for seven hours. As a mother of three children, one of them with health issues, I cannot even imagine the pain and grief of losing a newborn baby. For many people, it leaves a wound that never heals. For some couples, it can end the marriage. Maria and Stewart were told that their daughter's metabolic condition was so rare that the likelihood they would ever have another child with the same condition was very slim, so they got pregnant again. Their fourth child, Sam, was born with the same metabolic condition that Holly had. Miraculously, Sam survived. He is the first baby to survive his condition, and as joyful as that news is, the story doesn't end there. Maria and Stewart were so very grateful to have Sam, but they knew they had more to give, and they didn't want to take the chance of having another child with the same condition who might not survive. So they decided to adopt. As American doctors, they probably would have easily been able to adopt a child from the United States. Instead, they chose to adopt internationally, which was something Maria had dreamed of doing since childhood when she heard how baby girls were left to die in some cultures. She was determined to adopt a daughter of her own and make a positive difference in the world. Originally, Maria thought she would adopt from China, but after attending an adoption event, she and her husband both felt drawn to adopt from Guatemala. Their daughter, Gabriella, was born in February.

During her adoption process, the laws changed in Guatemala. It became more difficult for couples to adopt and take their adopted children out of the country. For Stewart and Maria, who had already met and fallen in love with their new daughter, leaving her behind was not an option. It took months of negotiations, tons upon tons of patience, prayer, and more than a little luck to get Gabby home for her first birthday.

When you talk to Maria about Holly, you realize that no child can ever replace another child, but you also realize something else. You realize that good can come from nearly any tragedy in life, including losing a child. There is, however, a much larger picture than a wealthy family adopting a child from a poor nation, because in Guatemala, as in many poor nations, human trafficking abounds. Gabby is a beautiful young girl from a very poor family in a very poor country, and there are people who would have offered Gabby's birth mother more money than she could have turned down to buy Gabby. Instead of meeting her friends at the corner of her cul-de-sac to get on the school bus together, she could be standing on a street corner, engaged in something no child should ever engage in. Not only have Stewart and Maria potentially saved a child from a life of horror, they have also helped her older sister go to college in Guatemala, which will hopefully break the cycle of poverty for her birth family. And if that weren't enough, every few years Maria takes her doctor's training and puts it to use for couple of weeks in a remote clinic in the back roads of Guatemala. She says it's her way of saying thank you to the people and the country of Guatemala for giving her Gabby. One of the most beautiful things that Maria says is that, if Holly had lived, they may have postponed adopting and would not have had the opportunity to have Gabby in their family, so Maria likes to think of Holly as Gabby's guardian angel.

Holly's short life here made Gabby's adoption possible. I can't think of anything more angelic than that.

MOTHERS OF ANGEL TEENS

Dear Mothers of Angel Teens,

This will most assuredly be the most difficult letter to write because you are the mothers none of us want to be, yet there you are. I hesitated writing this letter and considered leaving it out, but I think perhaps this is the most important letter of all because it reminds us of the fragility of what we do and how quickly life can change. You are the mothers who have had the rug pulled out from under you just when you were beginning to think you had made it. No mother ever wants to lose a child, especially the way you've lost yours. I pray you are surrounded by the support you need, even and most especially when you don't want it. I pray you find peace, but I struggle to find the words to help you with that. I stumble along in my own motherhood journey, thinking of you often, praying for you every time I do, and hoping beyond hope that you can find someone who is better equipped than I am to help you through the worst nightmare a mother can have.

I'm writing to you as a group because, although the circumstances of your lives and the lives of your children are different, you share the common bond of having them leave the earth just as they were beginning their promising adult lives. They were not young adults who died from acts committed while impaired by or addicted to drugs or alcohol. They did not fight a physical illness that robbed them of their lives. They were well loved and well raised by parents who loved them dearly and were a huge part of their lives. They were there one day and gone the next, leaving a hole in the life of everyone who knew them and a gaping chasm in the lives of those who loved them most. I cannot, nor do I want to, imagine your pain, but I have a small hope of knowing that other mothers are going through a grieving process like your own and knowing people remember you and your children often will provide you some small comfort. I know that for each of you there are days when you don't want to get out of bed and days when you haven't. I know that no matter how well you deal with the loss, it will always be there. I know that each of you comes from a background of faith, and although it may be the thing that sustains you on your worst days, it may not feel like enough.

There are so many things I want to tell each of you but don't know if it will comfort you or cause you more pain. I think that is why so many people say nothing—for fear of saying the wrong thing and adding to your sorrow, rather than relieving it. I fear the same thing but have decided to be brave and write from my heart, hoping the words will land on yours with the same love in which they leave mine. I wish I could give you five minutes—the five minutes before your children made a choice that changed the lives of so many forever. I wish I could give you the words in those five minutes that would have stopped them just long enough to change history, but I can't. Instead, I carry their memories in my mother's heart. I pray for them, for you, and for your families often. They flash before my eyes when my children achieve milestones, and I know that although you'll celebrate triumphs and milestones with your other children, you'll always think of the one who won't get those chances. Again, I hesitate to tell you that because I don't want to cause you pain, but I want you to know that your children live on, not just in your heart but in mine, as well. They are my inspiration to pay closer attention, to have more patience, and to be a better mother in every way.

My journey as a mother is not over, nor is yours. I pray that you find joy with your other children. I pray that you find peace in every day. I pray that you find yourself laughing a bit more every day as you honor your children by living well. Many years ago, I saw an episode of Dr. Phil counseling a woman whose daughter was murdered and was found in a trash heap with nothing on her body except a single earring. The mother was beside herself with grief and sorrow and could barely function. Dr. Phil asked her to describe her daughter, which she did with great affection. Afterward, Dr. Phil asked if her daughter would be pleased with the way the woman was living and dealing with her daughter's death, and the mother admitted her daughter would have been unhappy with her. Dr. Phil then asked the woman why she spent so much time mourning the moment of her daughter's death, rather than celebrating the years of her daughter's life. You could see the statement take hold of the woman as she realized that she had many more years of joy than she had moments of sorrow in her daughter's life. Several weeks later, when Dr. Phil brought the woman back on the show, she looked like a different person. She had decided she would celebrate the life and the laughter she loved so much about her daughter every day, and in the process, she had reconnected with the daughter she still had living in her home. Both felt like the mother had come back to life, and that, more than anything, is what I wish for each of you.

I cannot tell you who to be. I cannot tell you what to do. I can only wish and hope and pray that each of you will find the place where you can celebrate the life of each of your children; the aspiring engineer, the ever curious lover of science, and the beauty who loved nothing more than to help others. They inspire me. You inspire me, and they keep me humble as a parent, knowing that there but for the Grace of God go I. This mother's heart is forever changed because of each of your journeys and is better for having known about you and your children, and I am sure I am not alone.

I am humbled to share even a part of your story and hope that your stories will inspire so many others to become better mothers, as well.

With the greatest love and respect,

F or obvious purposes, I hope everyone understands why I do not share the details of the stories of these moms and their children. I stood in line at two of their children's funerals and grieved online with another. I truly struggled with whether to include this letter, but I read something that made me realize that this was important to share. It was a quote from a mother whose child had passed and said not to hesitate to mention the child's name because it might remind the parent of the child that passed. A mother never forgets about a child who has passed, but it helps that others remember, too. That is why this letter is included, and I hope that everyone who knows someone who has lost a child will carry that child in your heart and let the parents know how they positively affect your life. It is the best way to keep their child's memory alive and show support. If you can help, do so. If your help is rebuffed, understand that it has nothing to do with you and everything to do with a grieving parent's feelings. It's somewhere none of us want to be but those who are there need our thoughts, prayers, and support, no matter where they are in their grieving process, and if their situation inspires you to be better in any way, let them know that, too. I just did.

MOTHERING THROUGH GRIEF

Dear Elizabeth,

I knew I couldn't write a book about motherhood without including you. You have lived the life I could be living. I cannot imagine trying to raise two boys through their teen years without their dad present, yet you've done it, and you've done it well. There is so much I want to let you know: how much I admire you, how terrifying it was for me to follow your journey, how I silently celebrated when you found a new love. The things I could say about you would embarrass you, and that is certainly not my intention, but I think your story needs to be told for several reasons.

First, most people who got married two decades ago thought that they would be together for the rest of their lives. Few people thought about just getting a divorce if things didn't work out. They thought even less about losing a spouse to an illness, especially one that seemed to appear out of nowhere and change everything in the blink of an eye.

Second, we've discussed how people make an impact on others' lives, and you and Rob have both made a huge impact on mine and thousands more. Rob made his biggest impact on me through a short conversation we had about sports. He had just run his first marathon and was taking the day off from his elementary physical education position to rest and recuperate, but he had stopped into the office to take care of some school business. We walked out of the building together, and I mentioned my oldest son was starting tennis lessons after failing to make the junior high tennis team. He asked me if this was my son's first individual sport, and I said yes. He told me that he felt that every child needed to try an individual sport and a team sport, because the individual sport would give the child confidence that they could accomplish things on their own, and the team sport would teach them to work with others and be a leader. They were wise words that helped us guide our children through the world of sport and life in general.

In our day, marrying right after college was common. What wasn't common was spending every day together from the time dating started until years later as a married couple. It also wasn't uncommon for women to move from their parents' home to their new home with their new husband and set about living life as a married couple. Your plan was to be married for five years before you had a family; but within four years, you had two boys, fourteen months apart. Being a person of faith, I'm sure you will agree with me that the way to make God laugh is to tell Him your plans. I love how you say that the first year was difficult with two babies, but with the younger one striving to catch up to his older brother, that difficulty was short lived and your boys became best friends and playmates. It was an awesome time for everyone in your family, and you were having the time of your lives.

Your world changed when Rob was diagnosed with esophageal cancer and was given six weeks to live, and your boys were only 12 and 13. You made the very brave decision to set up a page on a website called CarePages.com and share not only the medical information that people who cared about you desperately wanted to hear, but also to make sure that the information in the public was factual and not embellished. The importance of that cannot be understated because Rob was a teacher in the school district he grew up in, and his mother had spent her career teaching in the same school district, as well. In addition, although Rob taught physical education at the elementary level, he coached at both the junior high and high school level, so the number of lives he touched was enormous. We all felt like we knew you on some level, though some knew you better than others. CarePages.com was a welcome line of communication for friends, family, and strangers and gave everyone the opportunity to send messages of encouragement, while still giving you some much-needed privacy. It became a vehicle for Rob to continue to teach through words, rather than through the physical realm, as he always had before. Instead of being in a physical classroom, he could share messages through his virtual classroom. When the Care Pages were no longer necessary, a family friend offered to compile all of the posts into a bound book and make it available for people who wanted it. It is not only a keepsake for your children, it is also a treasure to many who participated in its creation, especially since Rob was so inspiring and positive through every moment.

Before Rob passed, you two talked about everything. He even talked about the details of his funeral, beyond having a dear friend deliver his eulogy. He talked about how he would like his sons to wear suits but not black suits. He knew who he wanted as pallbearers. He told you to decide where the boys would go to high school since you had gone to private school and Rob had gone to public school. And he told you he wanted you to be happy. He wanted you to find love again. He did not want you to be alone or even stay in the home you lived in since it was Rob's family home and held so many memories of him. It was one of the requests that you wouldn't grant him, at least in the beginning, because it was also the home that your boys had grown up in, and you didn't want to uproot them from the only home they had ever known. You made changes so you and the boys could move on and plans to sell the house when the boys graduated from high school. The other thing that Rob didn't want was to be memorialized. You could not grant that because you did not always have control over the situation. There are scholarships, a yearly run, and a playground named after him. You understood that those are ways that others dealt with their grief, and you and your boys graciously allowed and supported those memorials.

I know your faith helped you and your boys face Rob's illness and passing with grace. You didn't realize until later that Rob's prognosis of six weeks, which actually became eight months, was not only a gift of extra time, but also the beginning of your grief process. You began to grieve the day the diagnosis became official. You will always remember the morning the doctor told you in front of everyone in the hospital waiting room that Rob had stage four esophageal cancer and there was nothing they could do for him, your husband who ran marathons, played tennis and kayaked, and was a Physical Education teacher who taught others to be healthy. Hearing that he was going to die was shocking, and the grief was overwhelming. Both of you tended to be private in your own lives, so sharing your story was difficult in the beginning, but as you learned lessons throughout your journey, you began to share those lessons publicly, which helped not only your sons, but the rest of us grieve in a better way.

For many people, losing a partner is devastating, and they fear they will be alone for the rest of their lives. For some, the idea of ever being married again feels foreign at best. For others, like you, who became a widow at 40, spending the rest of your life in mourning and alone was not appealing, especially when you and Rob had shared your journey on this earth so well. You said what you wanted and needed to say. You loved every day fully. You have a deeply held belief that you will meet again in a better place, and Rob had asked that you be happy and try to find love again.

Being open to a new relationship was not only natural, but it also honored the relationship you already had. After Rob passed, you went back to work, parented your very active boys, and spent time with families you had known since your boys were young. At one point, someone suggested that you try Match.com to ease back into the dating world. Although you weren't sure you were ready, you took a leap of faith and created your profile. After about six months and a few dates, you met Shawn and knew he was special and different. You also had a unique connection through grief. Shawn had his own grief story, one that helped him understand yours, which allows for space and/or comfort when it is needed.

You live a different life than many because you understand what is important in life and to each other. You have learned perspective. You are both slower to anger or become emotional or upset because you realize what you want your life to be every day. You say what you need to say and are able to live a peaceful, more anonymous life. While you are very grateful to the community you lived in for their incredible support during your grief process, you can now live life quietly without the mini-celebrity status that can make a private person uncomfortable. You know you have found the right man after having been married to the right man. You know that you lived well before and will continue to live well now and into the future. You are blessed.

Wishing you many years of marital bliss and blessings,

E lizabeth is an amazing woman. I know when she reads this she'll laugh her infectious laugh because she would probably say she's pretty ordinary, but that is what this book is about. It is about women who have lived well through extraordinary circumstances and become better people for it. So often when we grieve, we do it alone. We have support, but the majority of the time we are left alone to process our grief. Elizabeth and her family didn't have that luxury. Her husband and children were so beloved in our community that everyone felt as if they were part of their extended family. Everyone looked out for the boys. Everyone wanted to do something. It was kind and loving and noble, but at times it was overwhelming for the family.

As I said, Rob and Elizabeth ended well and left nothing unsaid. The boys spent time with their dad, and none of it was wasted. They lived fully and deeply and let go; and while they still have moments of grief to process, they are living and living well. Both of Elizabeth's boys are in college. She is adjusting to her new city and her new role as a live-in stepmom. It is a new adventure she is embracing fully. Life is not perfect, but it is very good, and that is the best that most of us can ask.

MOTHERS LIKE NO OTHERS

Dear Susie, Anna, and Lucy,

Some of the best mothering comes from those who have never given birth to their own children, adopted children, or even raised children. Maybe that's because you don't come with the baggage of being attached from birth. You build bonds outside of that. You choose to love rather than being bound by it. Whatever it is, you enrich the lives of those you touch, and the world benefits from your unique type of mothering.

Susie, you took in children from your own family without adopting them or taking away parental rights from those who gave birth to them. It wasn't easy to have their parents float in and out of their lives, leaving you to pick up the pieces when they were left behind or forgotten altogether. You loved them when they weren't lovable and gave them a life they never would have had otherwise. Now that they are grown and have children of their own, they understand the sacrifice you made. They all call you their mom and realize that birth does not always determine who "mom" is, even if they still call the woman who gave them birth mom, too. It gets complicated, but you muddle through; and the result is a dozen or more grandchildren who now without hesitation call you grandma, a name you wear well. It may not have been easy, but it certainly has been worth it, and the rest of your family thanks you for what you did.

Anna, you walk your talk as a Christian more than anyone I know. From loving stepchildren who, sometimes, were not happy to have you around to loving and caring for grandchildren who adore you, I've watched you mother when it was wanted and step back when it was needed. I've seen you endure some situations that would drive others crazy, especially when it has caused your loved ones pain. I've watched as you forgave more than some could bear because it kept peace in the family. I've watched you help raise your grandchildren with such love and grace, never accepting a dime for your service. It was my privilege to spend time with you when my children and your grandchildren were growing up. It was my children's privilege to share time with you and your grandchildren and have the joy of growing up with cousins. The memories we made together are special, and the memories they made at sleepovers at your house are still some of their favorites. Not many could do what you've done with as much grace as you've shown. I applaud you, and I learned more from you than you'll ever know, but the greatest gift of all is the privilege of calling you my friend.

Lucy, my friend, you remind me that people choose not to have children for many different reasons. I know much of your mothering instincts have been poured into your very lucky nieces and nephews. I also know that you have even found a way to spread that mothering energy around the world through a little thing we call the Internet.

It's easy to encounter negativity online. It takes more energy to find the positive, but when people who need mothering find you, they have found their way to an online home. You are a collector of tarnished souls. They seem to be attracted to you, maybe because they know you will show them love despite their transgressions. You lift the downtrodden. You show love to those who feel none. Sometimes they blossom, and sometimes they shrink away, not feeling worthy of the love you offer. I know your own heart has been broken a time or two, but you continue to lift others up and polish those tarnished souls. You believe in them, love on them, and find ways to connect with them through a screen, sometimes hundreds or thousands of miles away. You do sacred work through your virtual words. You show others a different way of being. Sometimes you see the fruits of your labor, and sometimes it seems as though you're banging your head against a brick wall, but you continue on.

To all of you, I am so grateful for what you have done for your loved ones in this world. I don't know if I could have accomplished what you have, but I appreciate what you give to those you love and can see the world is a better place because of it.

In humble admiration,

T he mothering skills of the women addressed in this letter have all made a difference in this world, even though none of them have ever given birth. Not all moms are created from a birth experience or adoption, sometimes they are created from necessity. In the case of Susie and Anna, they stepped in with family members when they were needed. They have provided food, shelter, and love to family members for the past two decades. They have made their way through more sticky family situations than most can imagine. They have kept their mouths shut when they wanted to scream. They have quietly gone about the business of doing what they have to do without looking for recognition, and their families have benefitted from it immensely. They approach life in very different ways, but they do it with a love of God and family that comes before all else.

Lucy is in the process of re-inventing herself and part of that reinvention is becoming a bit of a nontraditional mother. Lucy has a knack for connecting with struggling souls. These struggling souls seem to find her online and latch onto her kindness and sweetness. She accepts them and cares for them and encourages them through the screen, and in the beginning, they soak it up like a dried up sponge. She sees potential in them that perhaps no one else sees and offers them encouragement they might not get elsewhere. It is a wonderful gift that she gives to those who may have little positive input in their lives. The downside is that there is a tipping point where the recipient no longer feels worthy of the acceptance that is being offered.

Not many are raised with positive input. Most are raised in an environment where everyone points out where there is a need for change. It's especially easy to do that through an anonymous screen where there is no retaliation for ugliness. It is a much more difficult thing to bring light and positivity to the world, especially through an anonymous screen. Lucy has made it her passion to connect with those who yearn for it. She provides a safe place to vent with the goal of finding support, wisdom, and solutions to move forward in a positive way. She communicates privately with many, counseling, loving, and believing in them when they don't believe in themselves. It is a very nontraditional kind of mothering, but it has helped so many to move on in a positive way. Sometimes, she can say electronically the very thing a person wishes their own mother could say in person. It doesn't replace anyone, but it helps many.

Many women have taken on nontraditional mothering roles. Giving birth or adopting does not give anyone the ability to mother. It might even make it easier to see the recipient of the mothering more clearly without those histories and burdens. The impact these women have made in the lives of those they love cannot be overstated, and the world is a better place because they chose to love and mother in the ways that they have. It has been said that the world could be saved by the Western woman. We have a power unmatched in recent history, politically, financially, and socially. It is not time for us to take our place among our male peers and become like them. It is time for us to take the best of what we are and change the world. These women are doing that in a beautiful way, and it is a privilege to know them. They represent women around the world who take in those who need love and build them up to be something better. It is the essence of nurturing and mothering, and it is something we need so much more of in this world. I thank them for all they have done.

MOTHERING MY OWN
INNER BRAT/PRINCESS

Dear Pam and Nelly,

I can hardly tell you how much you have changed my life. Because of you, I met my inner princess, Ella. Ella had been a source of great frustration because she was a brat when I found her, and she has become a source of great joy as she has grown into the princess you promised she could be by following the path that the Divine has created for us. Pam, like you, I know that Ella isn't "real" in the sense that she isn't a live being, but also like you, I understand that Ella is a part of me, and once named, she became an integrated part of my life. She helps me grow to be a better person and occasionally leads me to an off-road adventure on my life's path.

I named my inner princess Ella because, when I met her, she seemed to have two very distinct sides to her personality and also because I'm a huge Disney fan. The scary side of her personality was demanding, unbending, wildly selfish, and downright mean. She reminded me more than I would like to admit of Cruella DeVille from the cartoon version of the Disney film 101 Dalmatians. There was another side of her, though, that was equally extraordinary. That side was kind and loving, giving and peaceful, and filled with the best traits of humanity. That side of her reminded me of Cinderella; thus, Ella was born, and so was our relationship.

Knowing Ella has let me explore exactly who I want to be and how I want to act. To think that came from just wanting to figure out how to keep my house clean is almost unbelievable to me. While taking a class in 2002, someone mentioned how FlyLady helped her change her life by teaching her how to keep a house. That led me to the FlyLady website, which led me to your books and eventually your website, and finally to you and to Nelly. You inspired FlyLady, and both of you have inspired me.

Pam, I know you have a sister, Peggy, who you love very much. I don't have a sister, but sometimes Ella and I pretend you are our older sister who shares her wisdom and helps make us better people. I remember the days we actually began to feel like we were grown up. We especially feel grown up when we talk to other people who struggle the way we used to. We know your life isn't perfect, just like ours isn't, but because of you, we are so much happier and have so much more control over our home and our lives. Even in those moments when things get out of order, we have a place to start and people we know are in our corner.

By getting our home, mostly, in order, I was able to write and publish my first book about parenting. As a stay-at-home mom, I've learned several tips and tricks and was able to share those in book form with those who were interested. It was a monumental effort, and Ella is part of the reason I was able to write the book in the first place. I could soothe her when she was frightened that her writing skills weren't good enough. I could assure her that even if only one person was helped, we did something good. We did get a letter from a reader who said the book changed her life. She told us she kept it next to her Bible and used both in her parenting. High praise, indeed, and we knew we accomplished what we set out to do. Now we're writing more books and blogging and creating more than ever because the real kids are growing up and don't need our everyday help as much as they used to. Two are in college and one is in high school, and we know our days of daily parenting will be over soon, so we are turning our attention to other pursuits. This book and these letters are part of that, and you and Nelly helped make that possible. We did the work, but you and FlyLady helped us clear the path to doing it without guilt. You taught us that we could keep and play house and have other pursuits, and we didn't have to clean all day every day. You taught us that when we took care of our homes on a daily basis, we could take time to play without guilt. Today, we play with words, and we love it just like you. We are proud to be who we are, and we are proud of what we have accomplished; but we needed help, and you were there with the kind firmness we needed. You inspired us to be better and stop beating ourselves up for what we hadn't done and focus on what we could do. You encouraged us every step of the way, and even better, you and FlyLady both encouraged us to adapt your system so it would work with our life. You gave us the steps, the structure, and the freedom to make it work for us, and it did. I never would have thought that getting that part of my life under control would lead to so much other success, but it did. It helped me to eventually address my financial mess and get that part of my life in order, which is an ongoing learning adventure, but this December, my oldest child will graduate with a degree in engineering, and he will graduate without any debt. I never knew that could happen until I began learning from you, and now it appears that dream will come true. The best part is that our second child began college this fall, and he is now in his second debt-free semester.

Now, I've also added taking good care of my body to my life. I'm just beginning to lean in to that after years of letting it go in some very unhealthy ways, but lately I've been keeping track, which seems to be my best way to stay aware of what I'm doing and change my behavior for the better. For instance, I've learned that after drinking 60 ounces or more of water, magic begins for me. Weight falls off easier, and I eat less. While I'm drinking, I am amply aware that there are many in this world who don't have access to 60 ounces of clean drinking water in a week, so I am focusing on gratitude, as well. I have found that a minimum of 7 hours of sleep is necessary for me to lose weight. When I get less, my body struggles, but I also know that my body tends to wake up at a certain time every morning, so going to bed earlier means more rest and a better chance of seeing the number go down on the scale.

I know it's not about the number, but the number helps me know if what I'm doing is working. You see, I had been calling my eating plan low carb for years, but I cheated, a lot. I blame Ella. In the past six months, I've logged my food intake, and the snacking began to disappear. I dropped 20 pounds in 10 weeks just because I began paying attention. Ella may have been unhappy about less snacking, but she was thrilled with 20 fewer pounds to lug around. Then the holidays came, and the tracking went by the wayside. Happily, I only gained about 5 pounds, but the bad eating was taking its toll. I was feeling awful, so after the holidays, I jumped back into a low carb and mostly no grain diet and things went in the right direction again. I felt better emotionally and physically. The aches and pains subsided and so did the grumps. Cruella was put in her place, and Princess Ella regained her throne. We have a long way to go, but because of what we have learned from you and Nelly, the detours are an inconvenience, rather than a reason to give up. We've watched our home go from chaotic and stress filled to nearly company ready and happy most of the time. We've watched our finances go from a constant fear of never having enough to prioritizing our spending and knowing we have enough to live each month, plan for large expenses, and even save some money along the way. It's a process of growth that we love most of the time because the peace we found in our home has made its way to our finances and is now on its way to helping us have the same in our body. Again, we are doing the work, but you and Nelly are our inspiration, and we are most grateful for that. You've been a constant source of positive input, even and maybe especially when we fail, backslide or feel like giving up. It took many years to get our act together and create a home we love to live in. It took about half that amount of time to get the finances together, and we're hoping it will take even less time to get the body in great working order. Our learning curve gets better because you've taught us to focus on the good and learn from the detours; and the faster we learn, the faster we get back on track, all because we took a class and looked at a website that blessed us more than we could have even imagined. Now you are inspiring yet another generation to get it together with www.thehousefairy.org for the kiddies and Www.cluborganized.com for the adults. Your websites are filled with teaching that helps us all make the world a better place and love ourselves a little more in the process. We cannot think of a better legacy to live, and that is part of what inspired this book.

Pam, I love the adventures Ella and I have had since meeting you and Nelly. I love knowing that we all have an inner child that can be a brat or a princess, depending upon how we treat her. I love that as a metaphor for life, as well. If we treat others like royalty instead of brats, we will see more regal behavior and fewer tantrums. Thank you so much for teaching me that lesson, and may you and Nelly continue to have more fun adventures than you can count.

Yours in fun and silliness,

P am Young is one of my "sheroes." She has changed my life in so many ways, and I hope someday I get to meet her so I can give her a big hug and express my thanks in person. I became acquainted with Pam and Peggy a few years after I began implementing the FlyLady system in my home. I got most of what FlyLady, aka Marla, was teaching, and my home had improved, but I felt like I was missing something that would help me pull everything together. When Marla was learning to get her home under control, the system by Pam and her sister, Peggy, provided the basics Marla needed to be successful and adapt the system for herself. While the FlyLady system had done that for me to a point, reading Pam and Peggy's books and learning their system made something click for me, and suddenly I was doing more in less time and making incredible progress. I live in a home I'm proud of now. I've learned to do the basics nearly every day so that if something comes up, I can skip a day or two of the basics and no one will notice. I've learned to do a little extra when I have the time, which means I never have to spring clean again. I've learned about the value of baby steps and a timer and allowing myself to be finished even when the job isn't done. I've learned to give up perfectionism, which leads to procrastination, and realize that allowing things to be good enough is sometimes the best path to success.

I do not know where or who I would be without these women in my life. They helped me learn skills my mother, who was organized at birth, could never teach me. They taught me be successful in an unorthodox way, which suited my unorthodox nature, and they helped me master housework in a fun way, which I thought was impossible. Then Pam wrote a funny book about taking care of finances called *The GOOD Book,* where GOOD stands for get out of debt, and I learned how to save money and become the fiscally responsible person I aspired to be. Then Pam wrote a book about losing weight. I've read it but have yet to fully integrate it into my life; however, I am 30 pounds lighter than I was 6 months ago, so I'm on my way. Who knows where they might lead me in the future, but by following Pam's encouraging advice, I'm sure it will be fun.

VIRTUAL MOTHERS

Hello Lovelies,

I'm not sure how to talk about all of you. We are the strangest of communities, and I wasn't sure whether a letter about our communities belonged in a book about motherhood, but I think you'll agree in the end that it does. For one group, our crazy beginning is the result of wanting to be better at taking care of our homes, which led us to the FlyLady website. I'm not sure any of us would have ever crossed paths any other way since we're from California, Florida, Georgia, Kansas, Kentucky, Idaho, Indiana, Illinois, Kentucky, Maine, Massachusetts, Minnesota, New Jersey, Ohio, Oregon, Texas, Utah, Washington, West Virginia, and Wisconsin in the United States. We're also from Australia, Canada, England, Finland, and New Zealand, making us quite an international group. We range in age from the 20s to the 60s. We were connected initially in a chat room that often went off the grid, so we moved to a private group on Facebook, which became so much more than a group that cheers one

129

another on to a cleaner home, although several of us have finally figured that piece out, as well.

We've seen each other at our best and our worst, and perhaps we work so well because we don't have to face each other at our worst. We can vent. We can be angry. We can let our ugly out, and now and then, we've even turned that ugly on one another. We've had disagreements and spats. We've had members leave the group peacefully, and we've had members disagree vehemently and choose to no longer communicate with one another. It reminds me of so many families, but even in our worst moments or shortly after, there is usually forgiveness. We get over the hurt feelings; and even when we don't, we can all rally around the next member that needs us. We have celebrated marriages and births, new homes and travel, new jobs, and sending children off to college and kindergarten. We've also ached with our sisters through parenting and spousal struggles, financial fears, health challenges, and more. We keep those struggles private because the group gives us a safe place where it's okay not to be okay. The older members mentor and mother the younger ones. The younger ones lighten up the older ones. For those of us who are mothers, I believe every one of us is a better mother because we are a part of this group, and not only do we mother our own children better, we mother each other better, as well. We send virtual hugs and loving sentiments. We send real gifts. Occasionally, we even get to meet in person, and the world opens up to all of us even more.

Many people will say that online friends are not really friends because they can be anyone they choose to be, but we've been who we are and sometimes who we don't want to be. We've been tired and mean and sarcastic and broken. We've been down so low we thought we might never get up again, and every time, when we bring our sadness and brokenness to the group, we are lifted and hugged back to a better place. We are not fixed, and some of our issues are too big to ever be fixed through a screen, but we know someone cares. We know someone has listened to our pain and will walk through it with us, especially when we feel we cannot share that pain with those in our off-screen lives. I have never been so thoroughly mothered as I have by the women in this group. They bring every perspective imaginable, from straight talk to incredible humor. We have spunk and grace, humor and wit, wisdom and love, and we have each other.

When we have a problem, many of us turn to the group first, and someone will invariably have an insight we wouldn't have thought of or considered. It isn't always what we want to hear, but it's often what we need to hear, and after the sting wears off, we move on with our lives. We are all better for having been part of this group and part of each other's lives, and that's what friends are for, no matter how they walk through this life. I know I've said several times how much I love and admire the women in our group, but this time I get to say it to the world. What we have is special. What we have is amazing, and I hope we get to continue having it for a very, very long time.

Hugs and love,

There is so much craziness online or so they say, whoever "they" are, but I have been blessed with some of the most positive influences in my life from online resources, and this group is right at the top. I am part of several groups that are designed to improve people's lives. I am a member of a creativity salon in which creative souls encourage each other to create their best product, no matter what type of art they make. I am part of a writer's group that focuses on helping writers succeed in the creation and marketing of their work, and this group will definitely be helping me finish and market this book. I also belong to the private group I addressed above. Other than monitoring my children on Facebook, this group was the biggest reason I became active on social media. The members are such a cross section of women, from those who hunt their own food to those who would never pick up a gun. They are members of several religions and no religion at all. Some have no children, and some are mothers to as many as six. Their financial status ranges from having nearly no money to being financially secure. They are so very different; yet, the page is an incredibly safe place to vent, be angry, and find our way back to a better version of ourselves. It is my hope that everyone, especially mothers who crave support, can find a place like this to feel the support and get the guidance we all sometimes need. The groups are there, and the longer I participate in this mix we call social media, the more special those with a positive message mean to me. They inspire me to live better and evolve into the best mom and person I can possibly be. They are a gift. They are amazing, and I am incredibly blessed to be part of their lives and have them in mine.

CONCLUSION

Years ago, I thought being "just a mom" wasn't enough. I thought there was more to life, but at the same time, I loved being a mom more than any job I had ever had. Nothing made me happier than hanging out with my family, snuggling with my babies, and creating a happy home for those I love most. I saw other moms living different lives and wondered if I was doing something wrong, but as my children grew and I talked to more and more moms, I realized that we all ask the same questions. We all wonder if we're doing a good job or could do better. We are all trying our best, and even those who do an extraordinary job don't always get the support they need. Still, we all keep mothering the best we can. Nothing makes me happier than when my husband and kids tell me I'm doing a great job as a mom and wife. I'm the only female in our home; as you can imagine, those compliments don't come often in a house full of males. I understand, but I love it when I hear it. Because I love it so much, I want other moms to hear it from me or, in this case, read it.

The women in this book were all surprised to learn that I wanted to include them. None of them see themselves as heroic, though I do, and most of them didn't know I was paying such close attention. Luckily, they let me share their stories anyway. I hope every one of them knows that this a snapshot of their lives. None of them has had it easy. All of them have worked hard to be who they are. They have good days and bad days, but they've all done something to inspire me to be a better mom, and I hope that they will do the same for everyone who reads this book.

It is also my hope that everyone will take a few moments out of their busy lives to send a letter to someone who has influenced them in a positive way. Love Letters to Moms Day (May 6) is the perfect opportunity to honor those people in your life, whether they are your mom or someone you admire. Like some of the women you've read about in this book, not all moms are traditional, but all moms could use recognition and appreciation. Whether you participate in Love Letters to Moms Day or select another time to share your sentiments, it's never too late to send your own love letter to someone who mothered you or inspired you to be a better person.

Being a mom has been the greatest spiritual adventure of my life. I know it isn't for everyone, but it is definitely for me. If you are a mom, want to be a mom, have pretended you are a mom, or even had a mom, reach out to another mom or mom figure and let them know how much they mean to you. You never know where it might lead.

To contact or follow Karen Bemmes, you can use the following links.

- Facebook: https://www.facebook.com/karen.bemmes?fref =ts

- Twitter: https://twitter.com/pkbemmes

- YouTube: https://www.youtube.com/channel/UCQsC8-ZYX5JRaSUkYCL984w

- LinkedIn: https://www.linkedin.com/in/karen-bemmes-2787459?trk=hp-identity-name

- Wordpress: https://wordpress.com/posts/karenbemmes.wordpress.com

- Website: www.pkbemmes.com